Art to Hear

# The Master of Flémalle and Rogier van der Weyden

HATJE
CANTZ

Städel Museum«

# CD Index

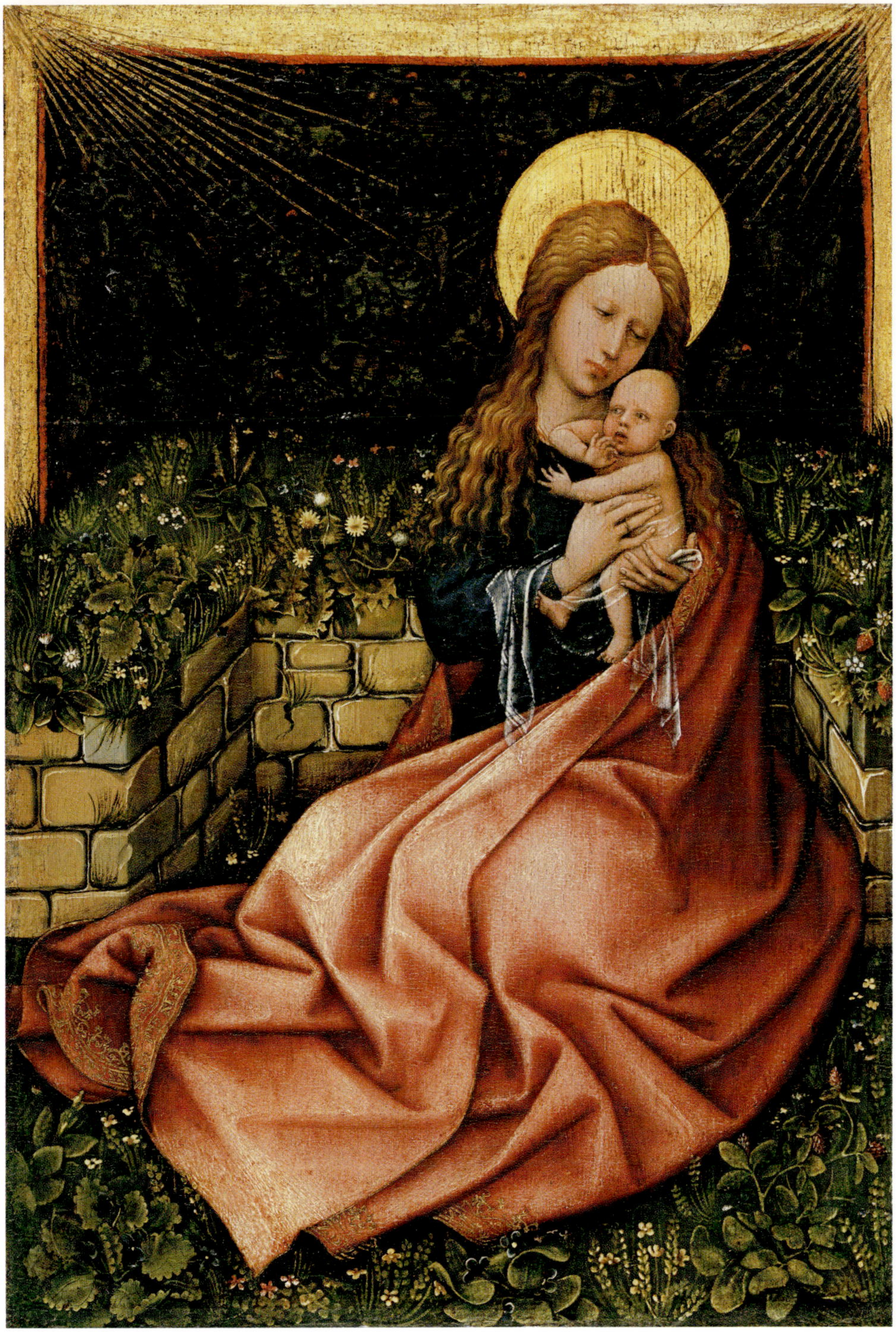

▷ 2 Master of Flémalle Madonna by a Grassy Bank Staatliche Museen, Gemäldegalerie, Berlin

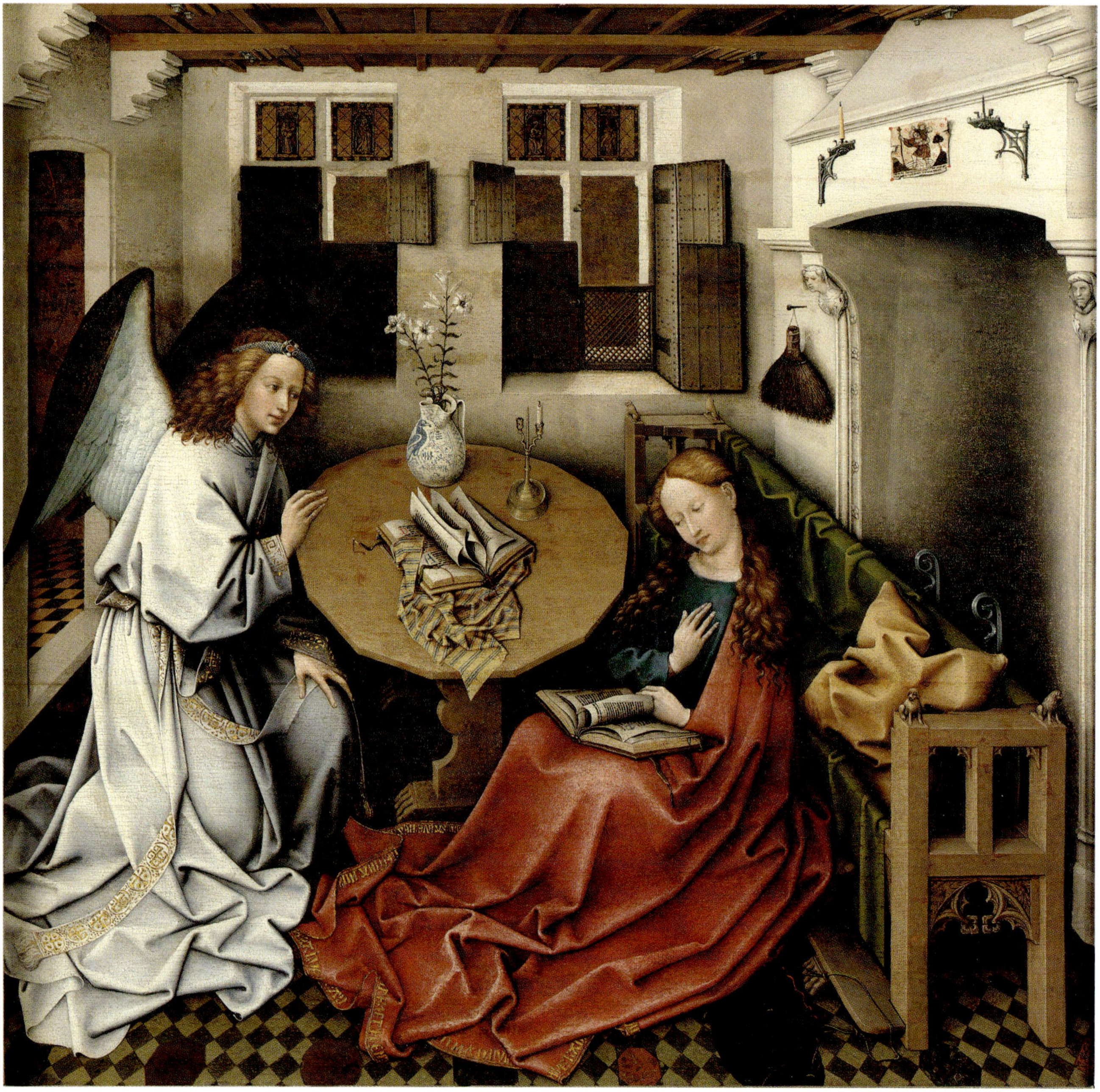

 ▷ 3 Master of Flémalle The Annunciation of the Virgin Musées Royaux des Beaux-Arts de Belgique, Brussels

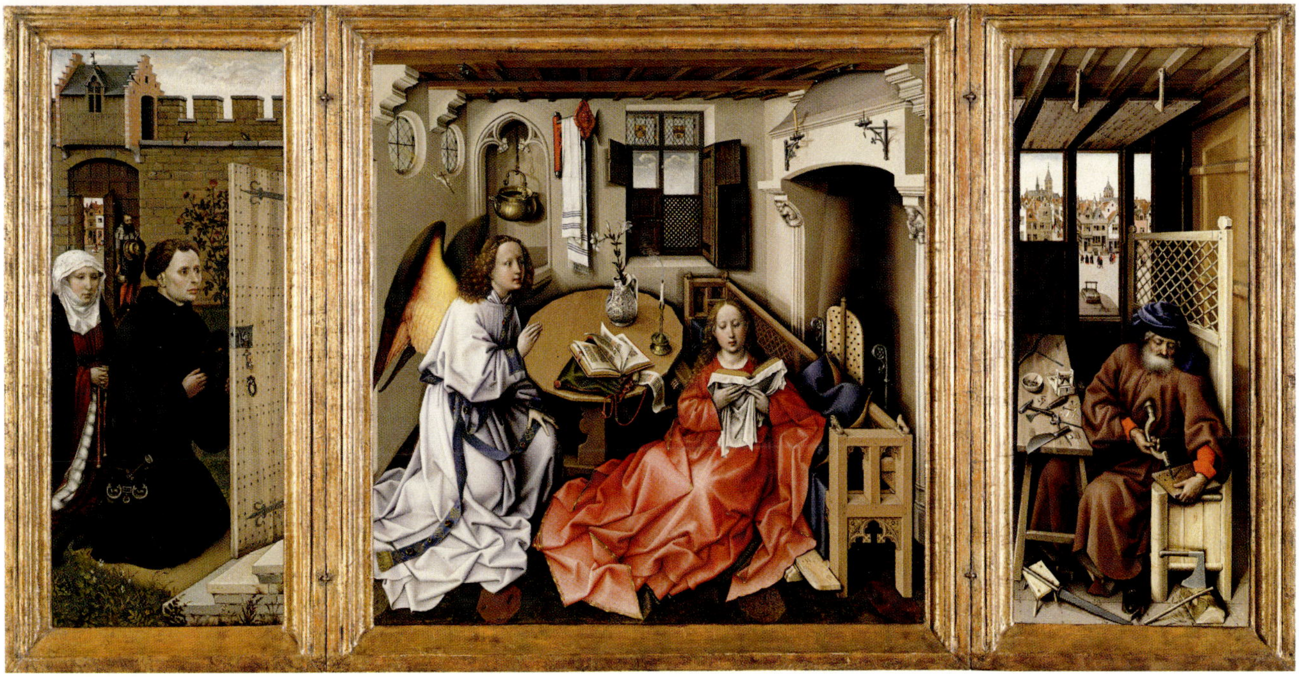

▷ 3 **Master of Flémalle** Mérode Triptych The Metropolitan Museum of Art (The Cloisters Collection), New York

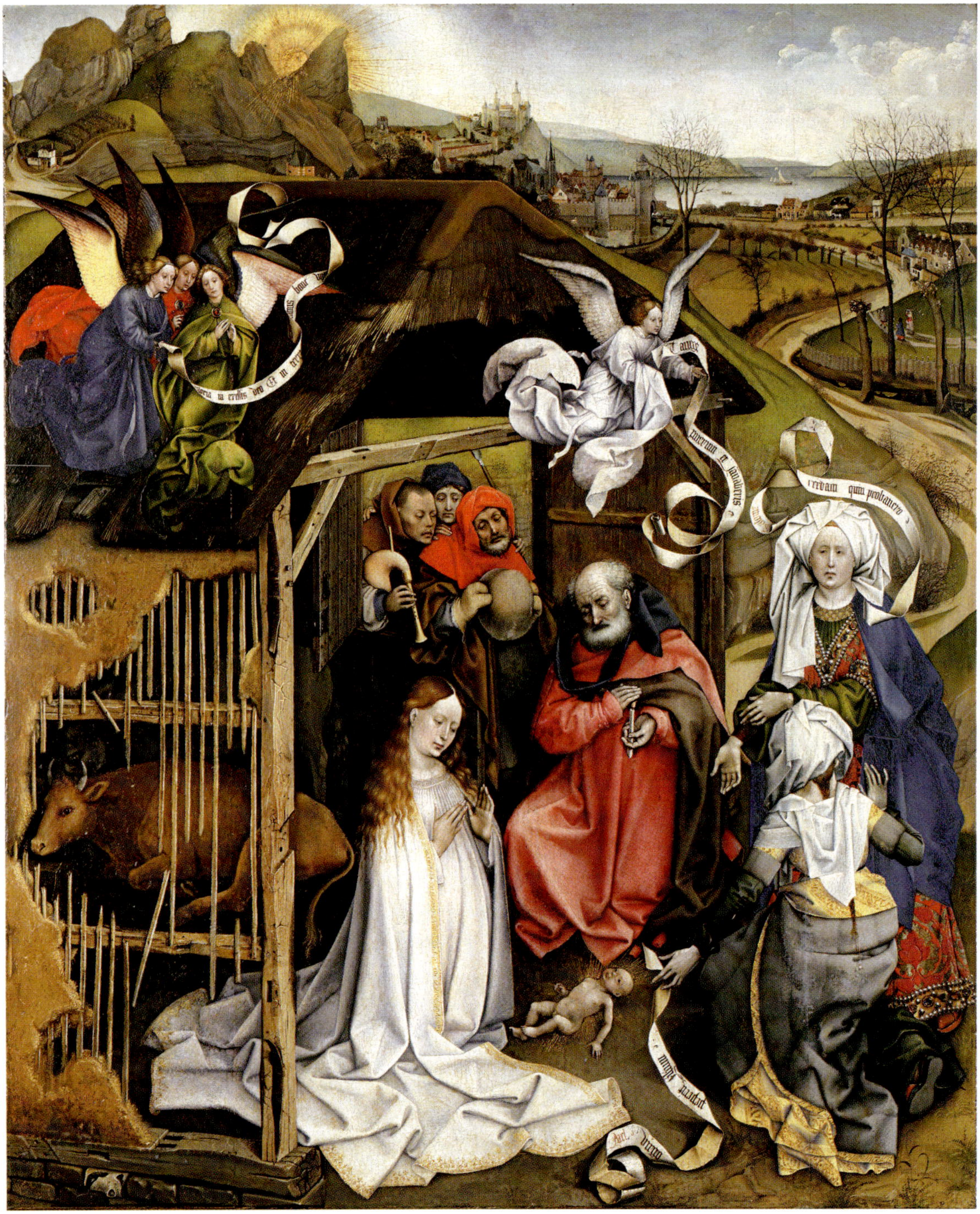

▷ 5 **Master of Flémalle** The Nativity Musée des Beaux-Arts, Dijon

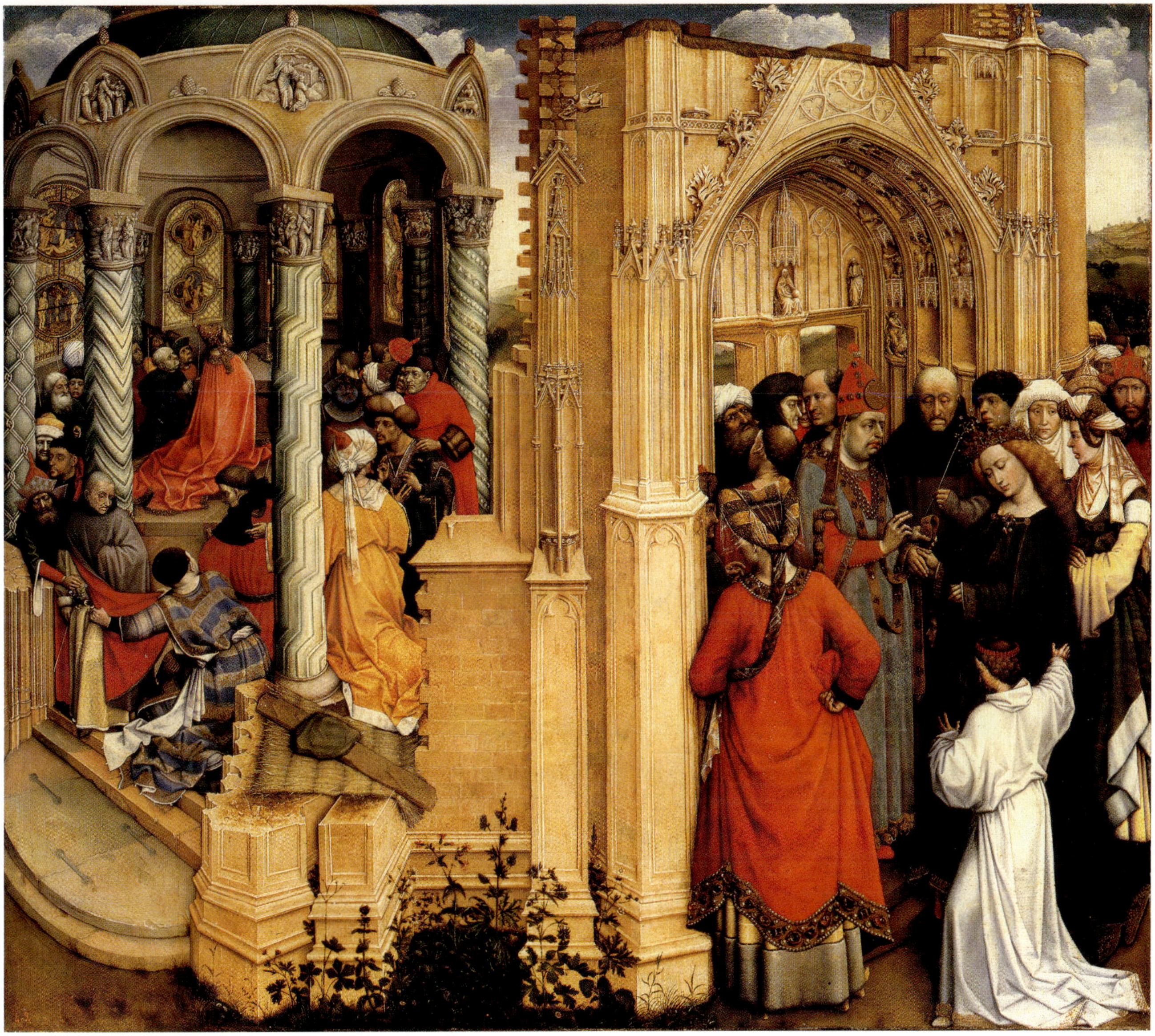

▷ 7 Master of Flémalle The Miracle of the Rod and the Marriage of the Virgin Museo del Prado, Madrid

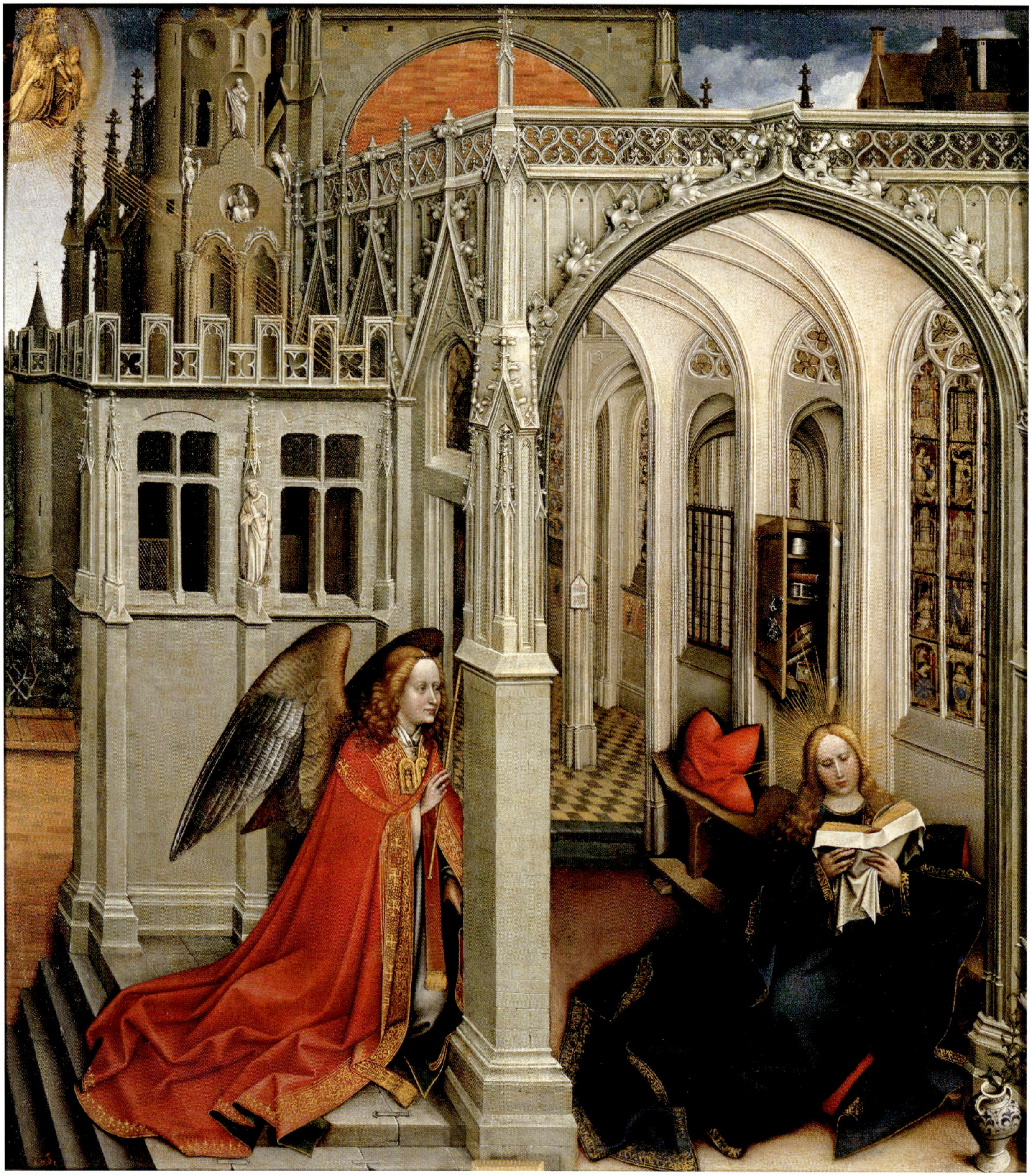

 ▷ 7 Master of Flémalle The Annunciation of the Virgin Museo del Prado, Madrid

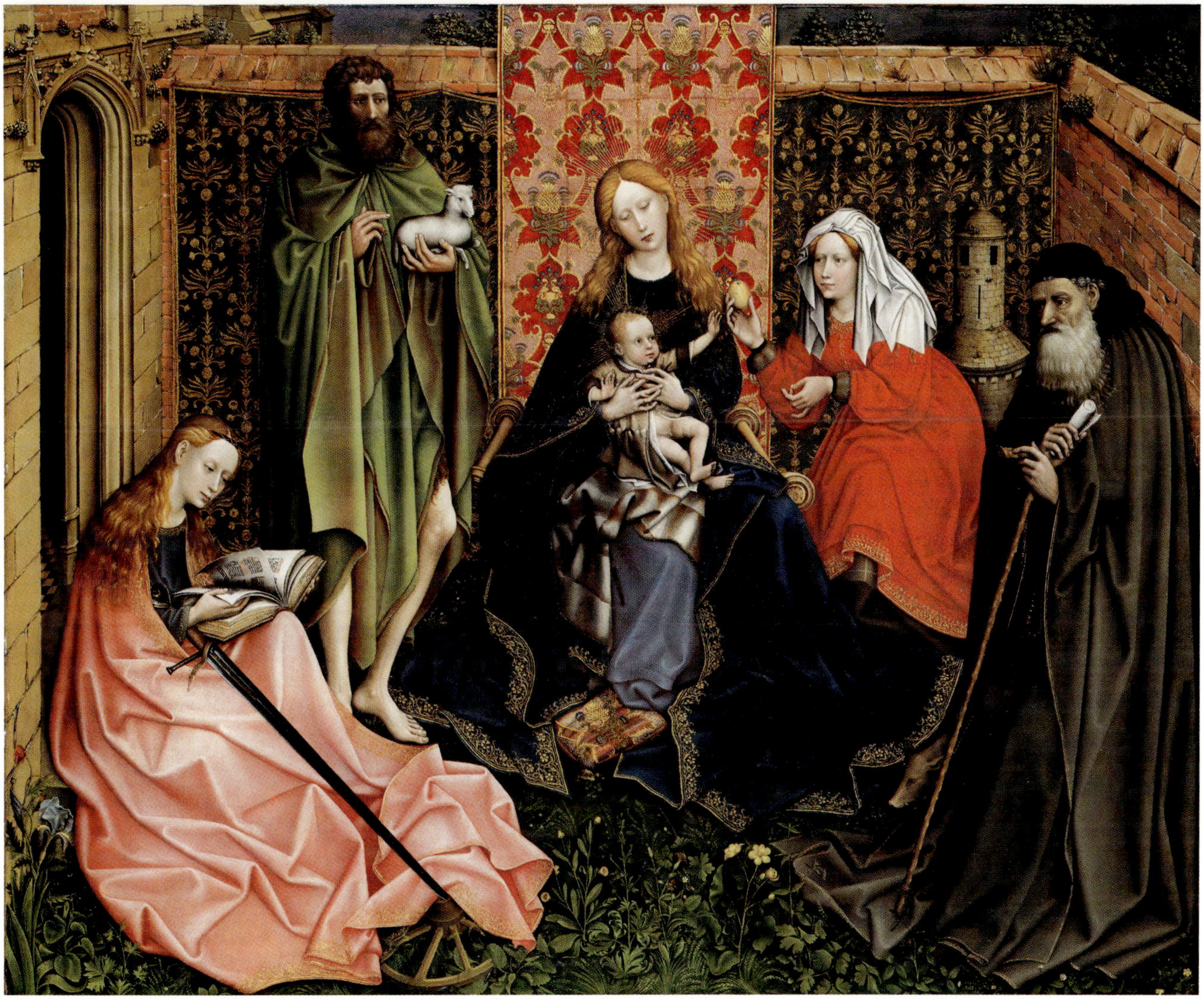

▷ 9 Master of Flémalle Madonna with Saints in a Garden National Gallery of Art, Washington, D.C.

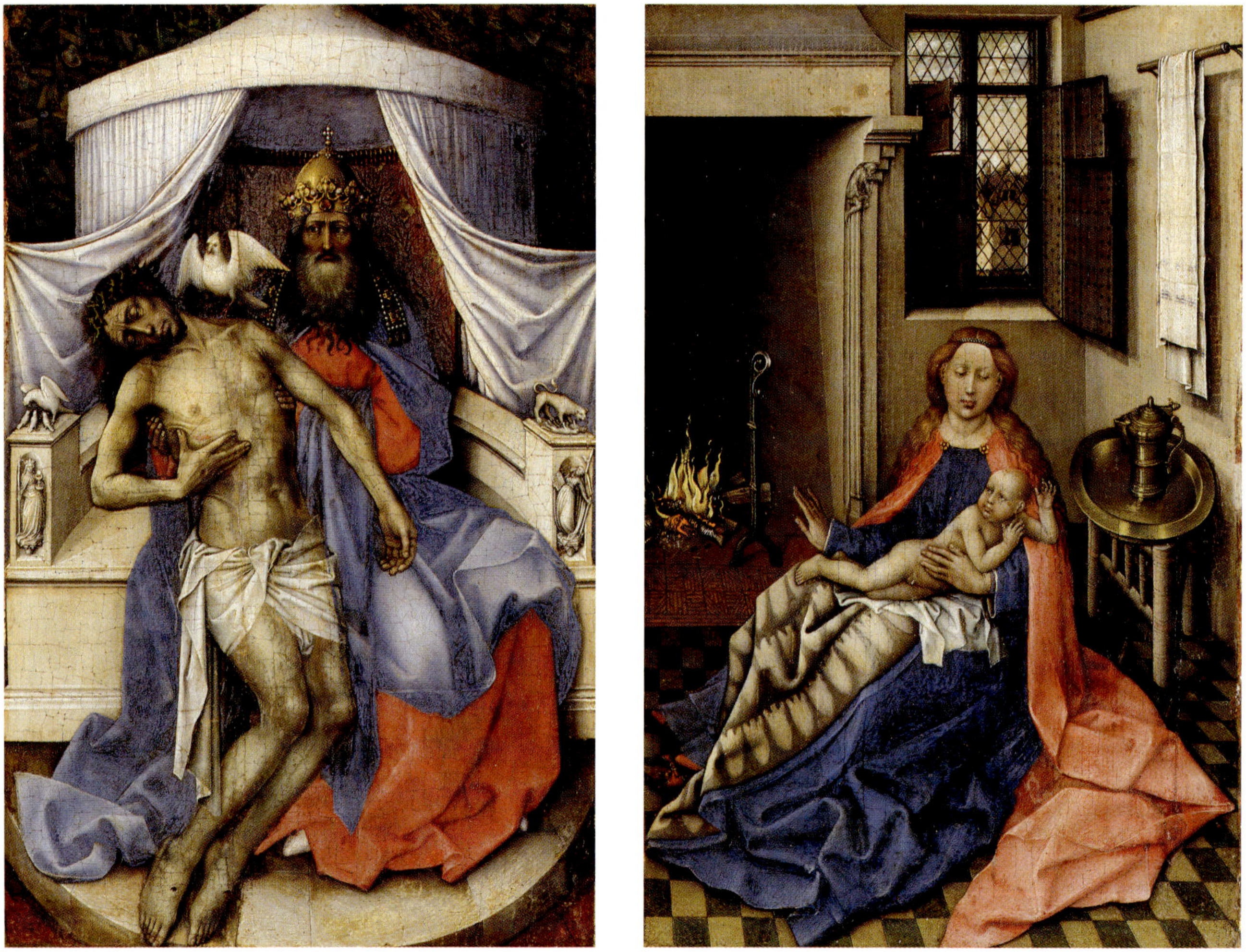

 ▷ 10 Master of Flémalle Diptych with the Madonna and the Throne of Grace Trinity The State Hermitage, St. Petersburg

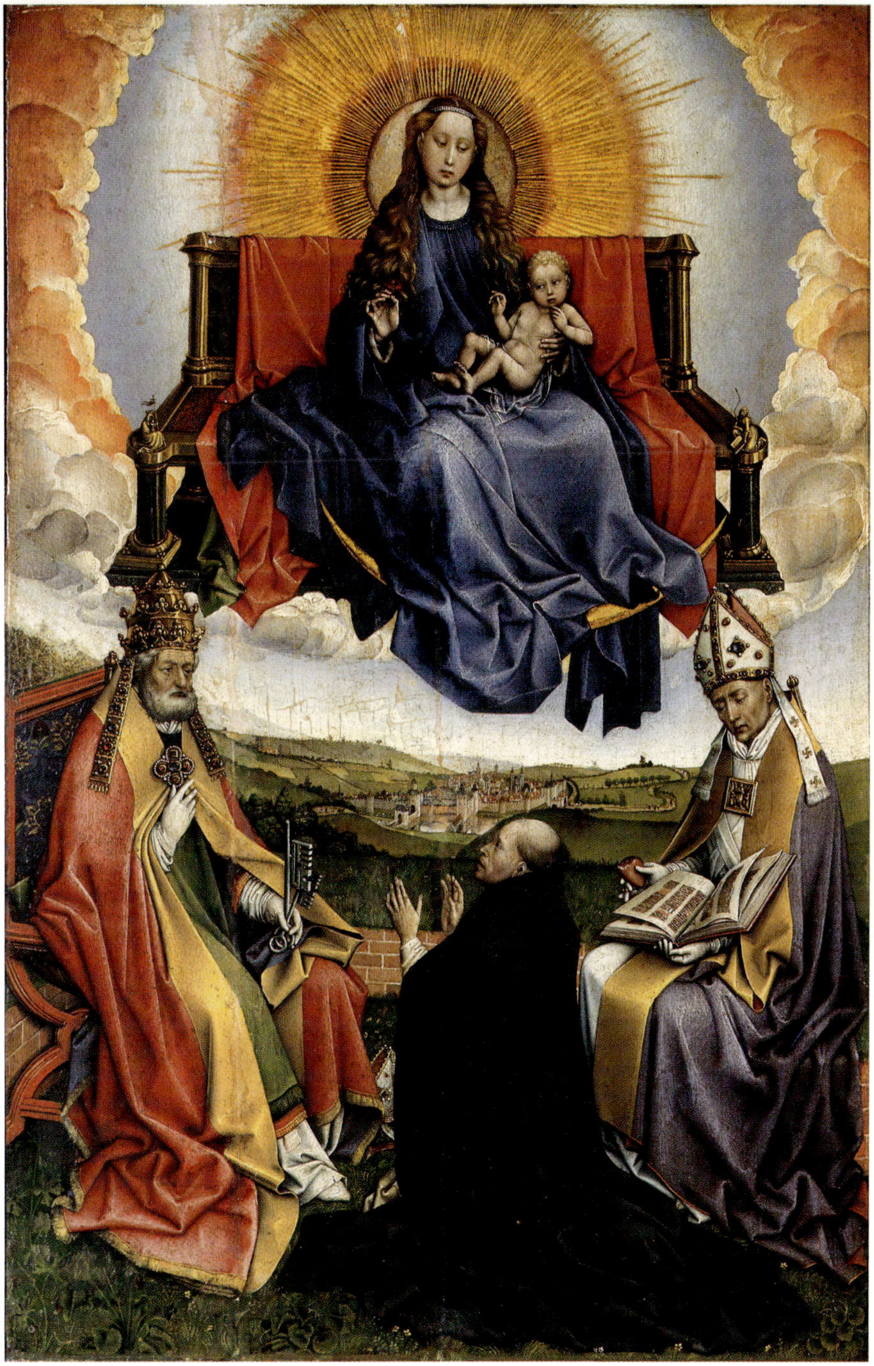

▷ 11 Master of Flémalle The Virgin in Glory Between Saint Peter and Saint Augustine and Venerated by a Donor
Musée Granet, Aix-en-Provence

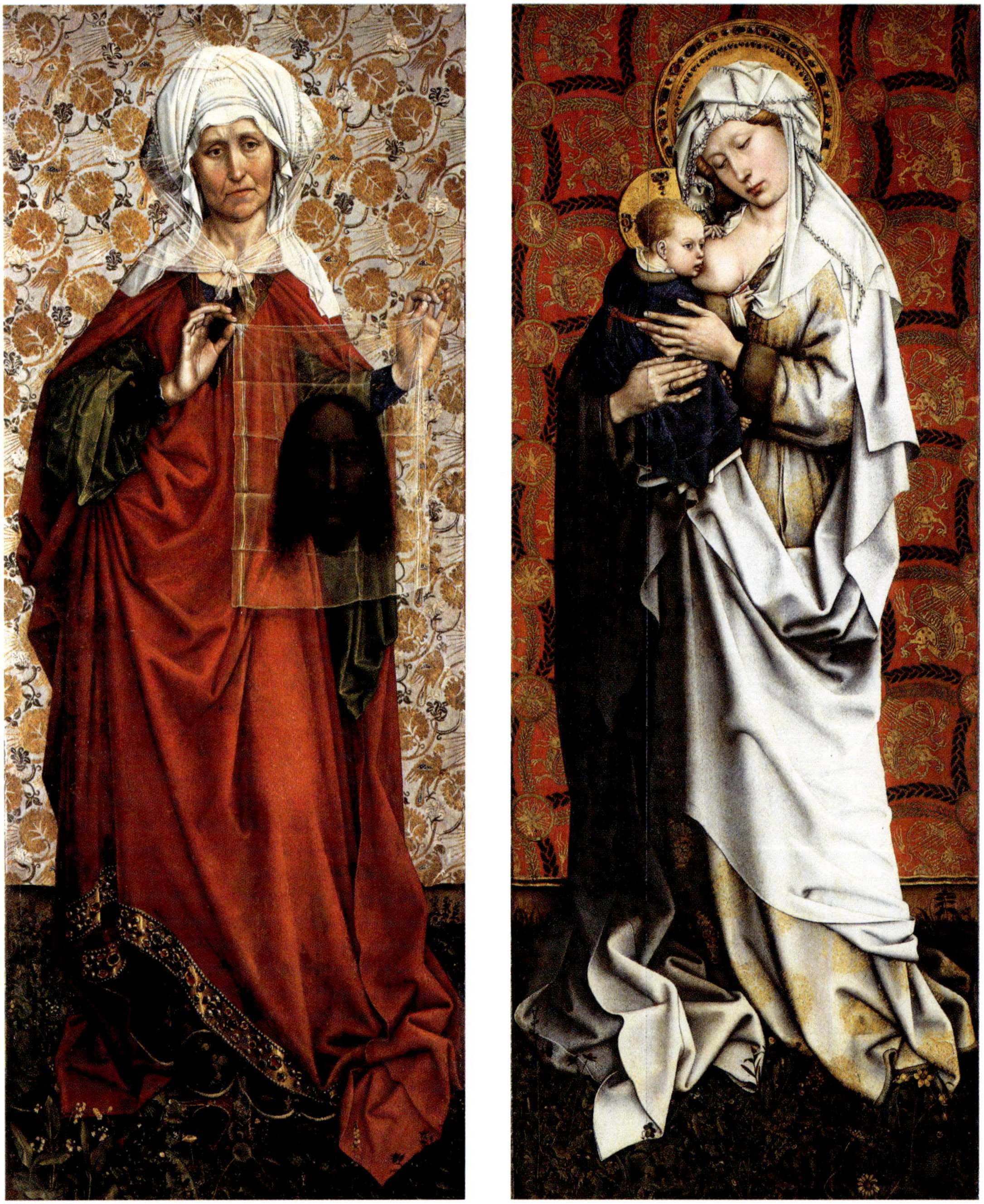

▷ 12 Master of Flémalle "Flémalle Panels":
Saint Veronica with Her Cloth
The Virgin Mary Nursing the Infant Jesus Städel Museum, Frankfurt am Main

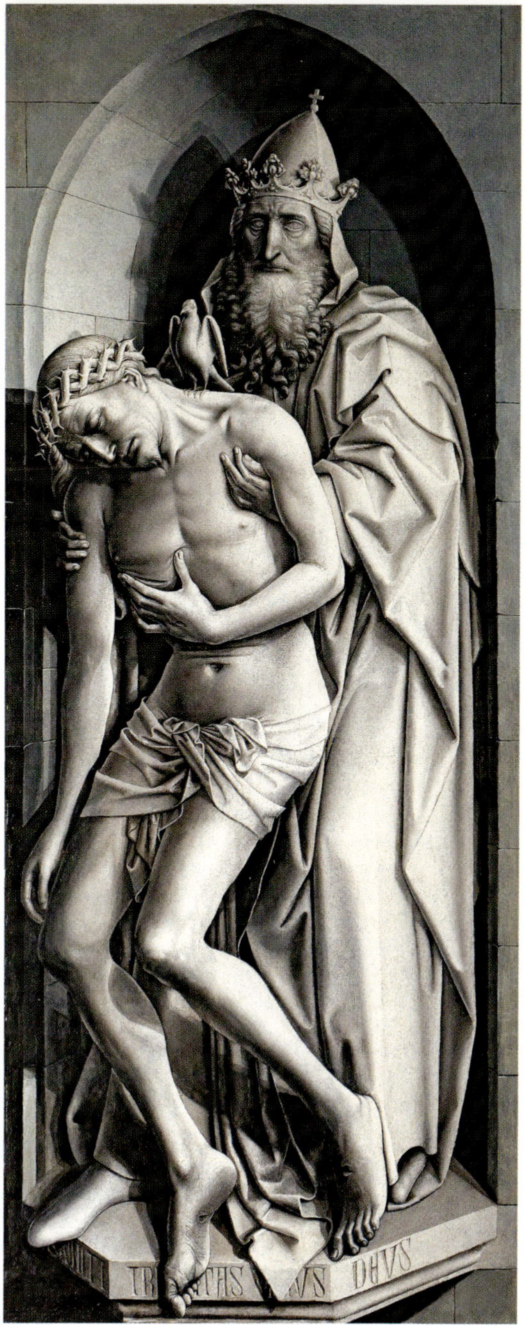

▷ 12 Master of Flémalle "Flémalle Panels": The Trinity Städel Museum, Frankfurt am Main

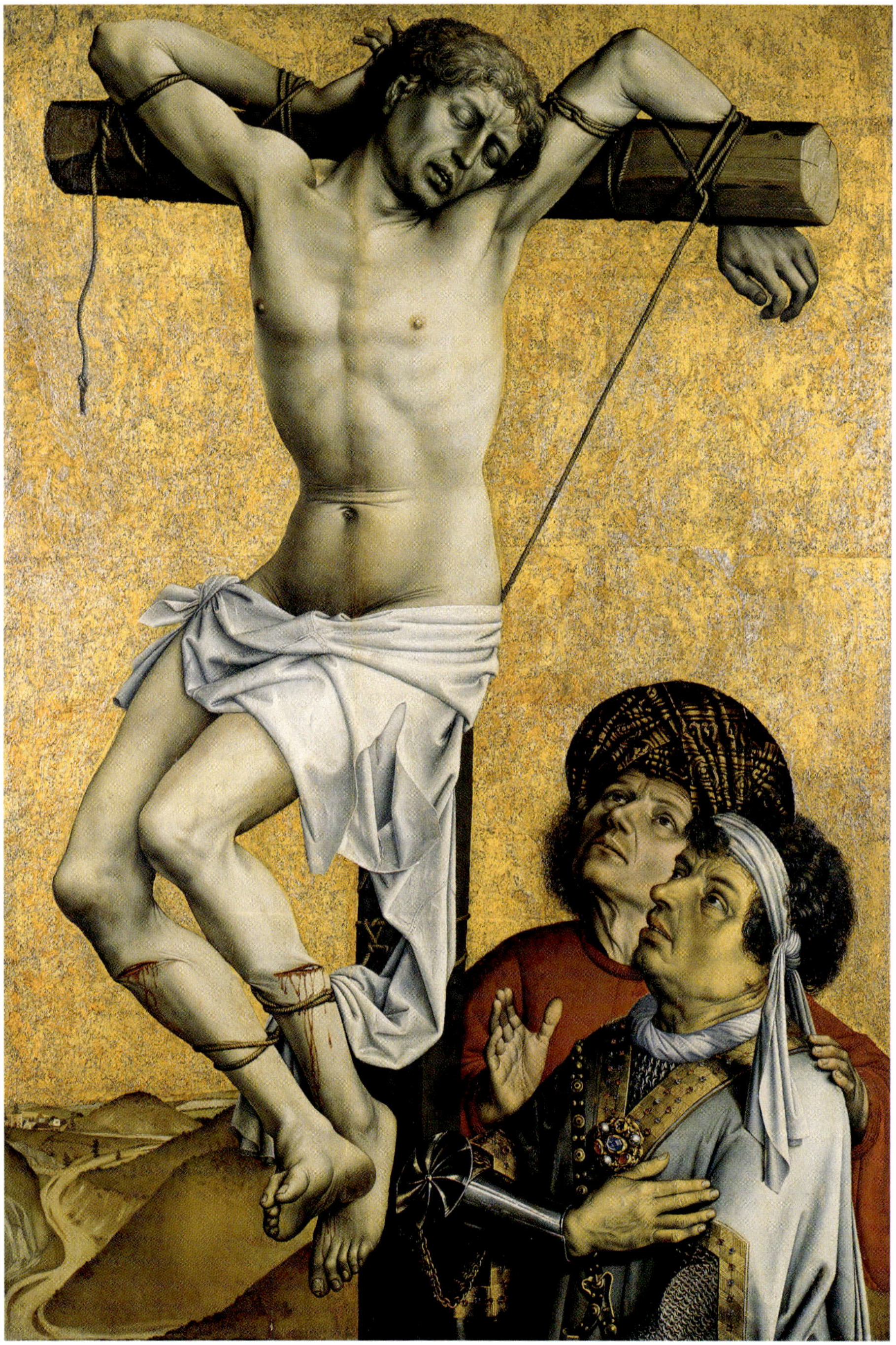

▷ 13 Master of Flémalle Fragment of an altarpiece wing painted on both sides:
The Bad Thief to the Left of Christ Städel Museum, Frankfurt am Main

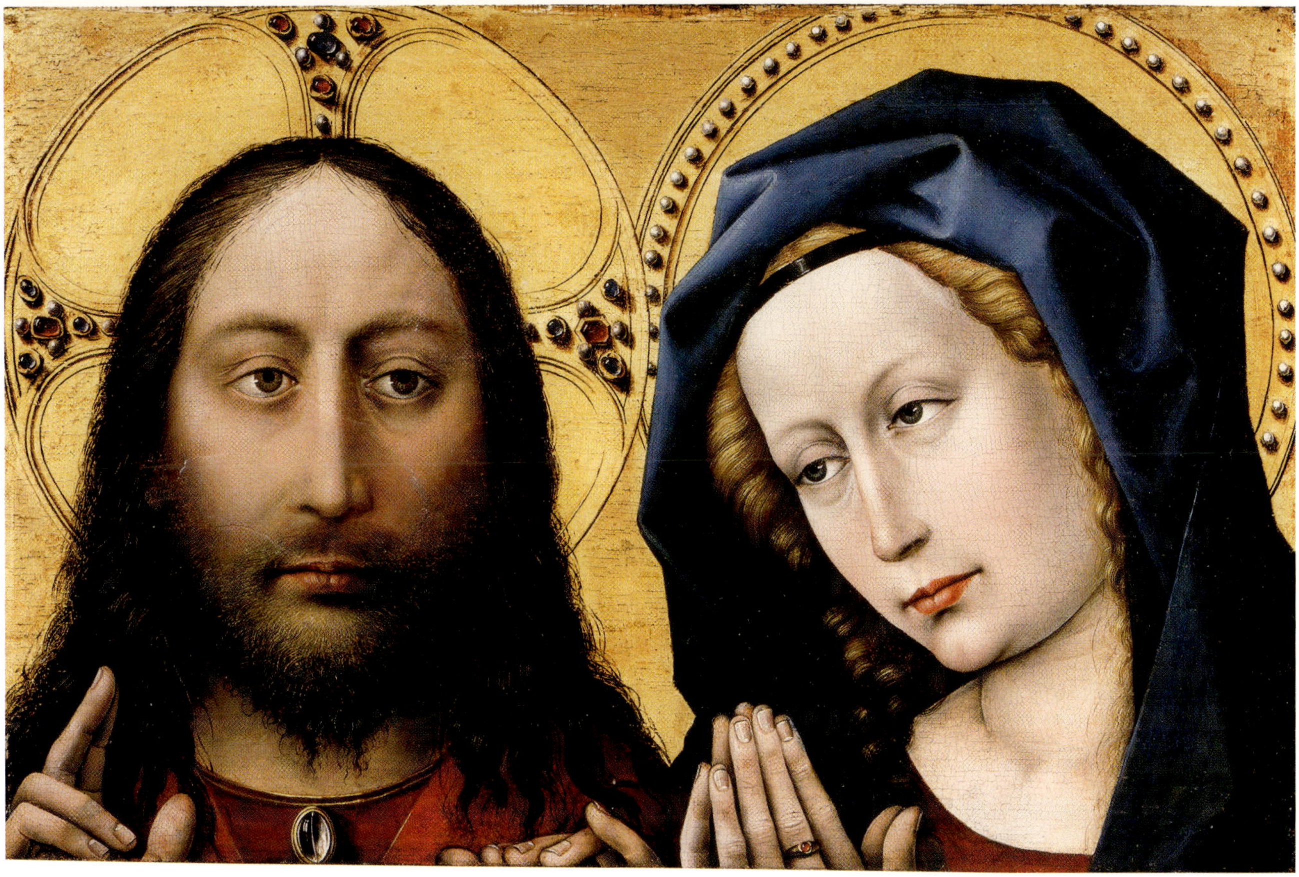

▷ 14 Master of Flémalle Christ and the Virgin Philadelphia Museum of Art, Philadelphia

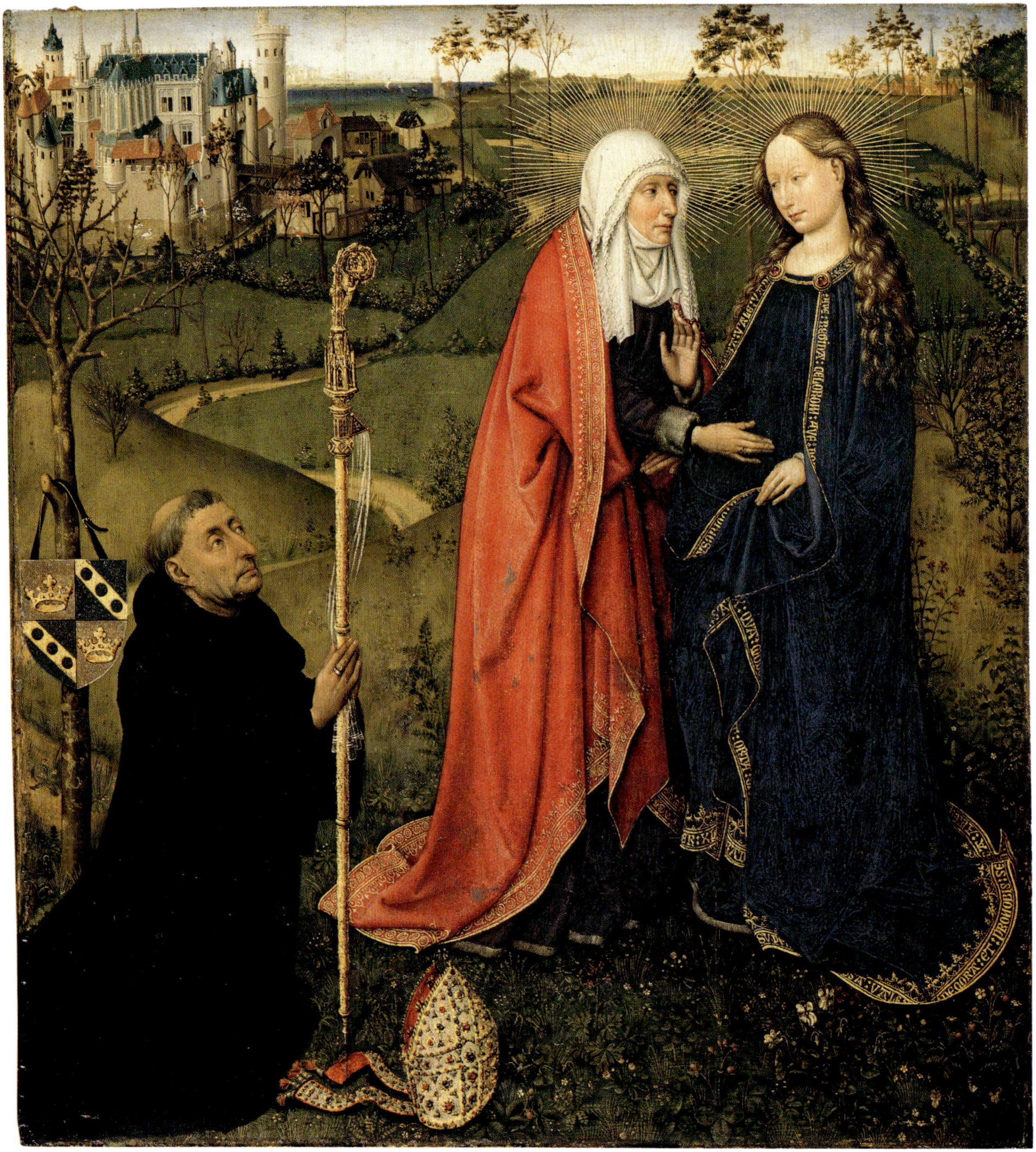

▷ 15 **Jacques Daret** Four panels of the altar of Saint Mary from Saint-Vaast in Arras: The Visitation
Staatliche Museen, Gemäldegalerie, Berlin

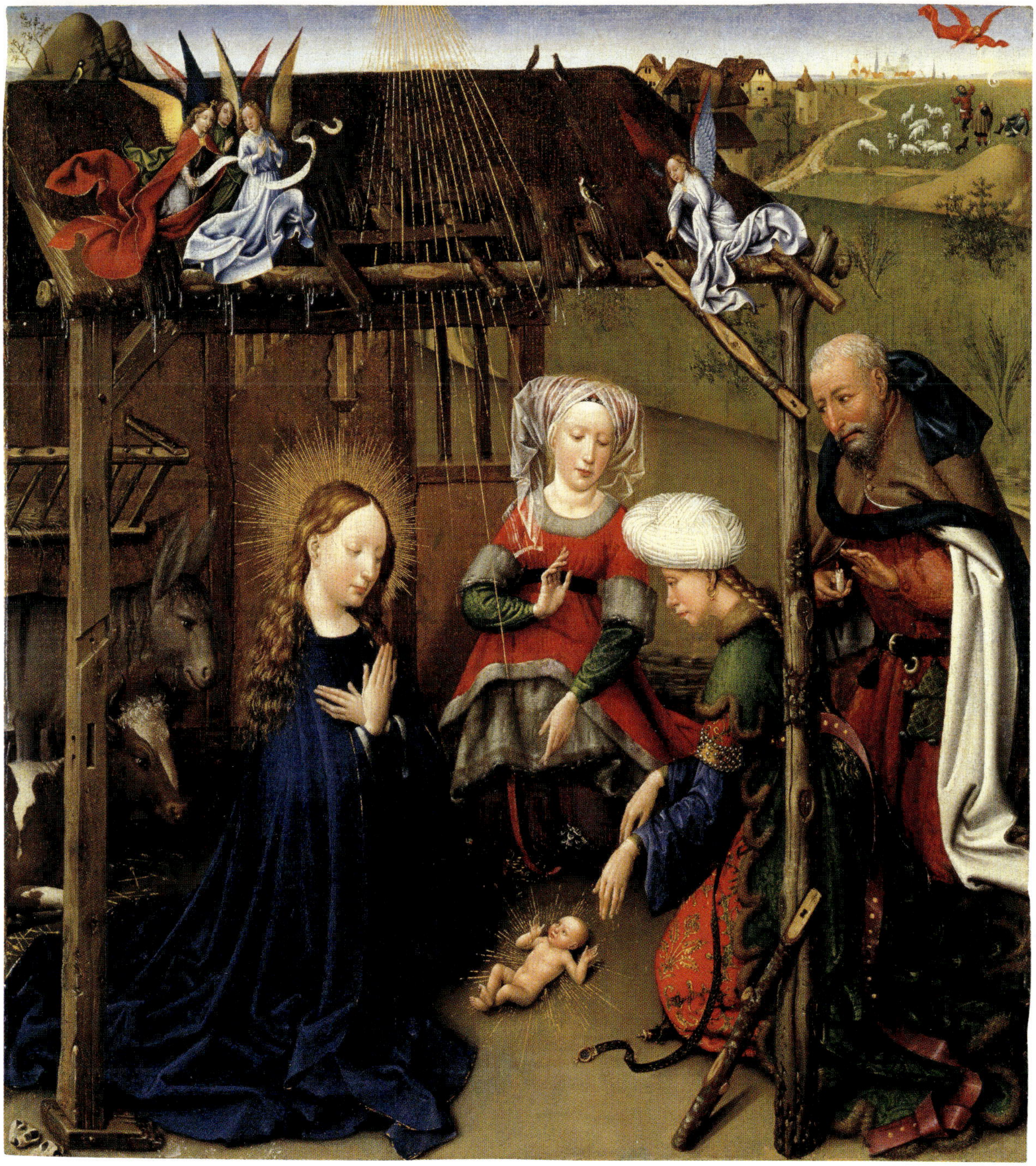

▷ 15 **Jacques Daret** Four panels of the altar of Saint Mary from Saint-Vaast in Arras: The Nativity
Museo Thyssen-Bornemisza, Madrid

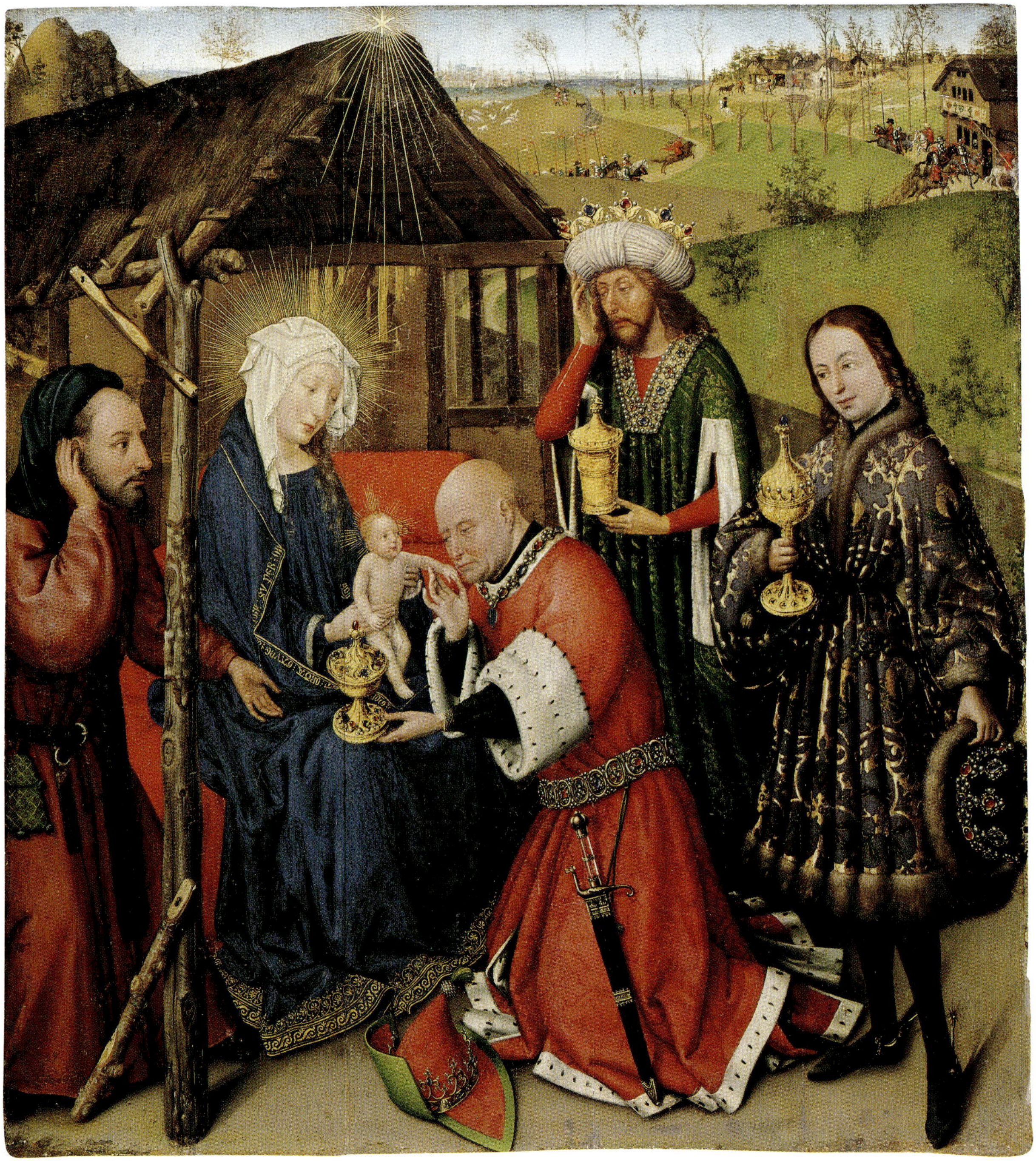

▷ 15 Jacques Daret Four panels of the altar of Saint Mary from Saint-Vaast in Arras: The Adoration of the Magi
Staatliche Museen, Gemäldegalerie, Berlin

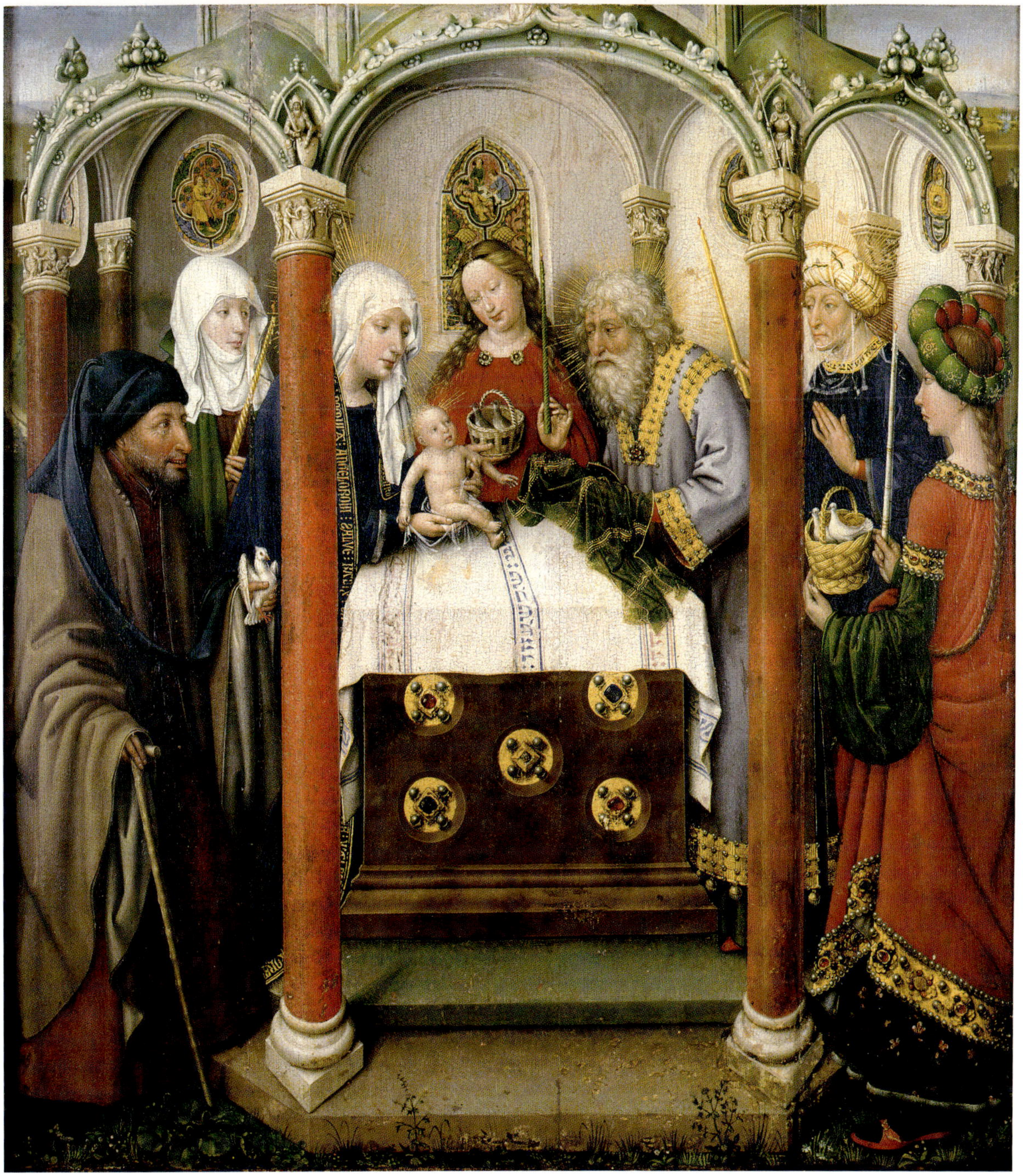

▷ 15 Jacques Daret Four panels of the altar of Saint Mary from Saint-Vaast in Arras: The Presentation
Musée du Petit Palais, Paris

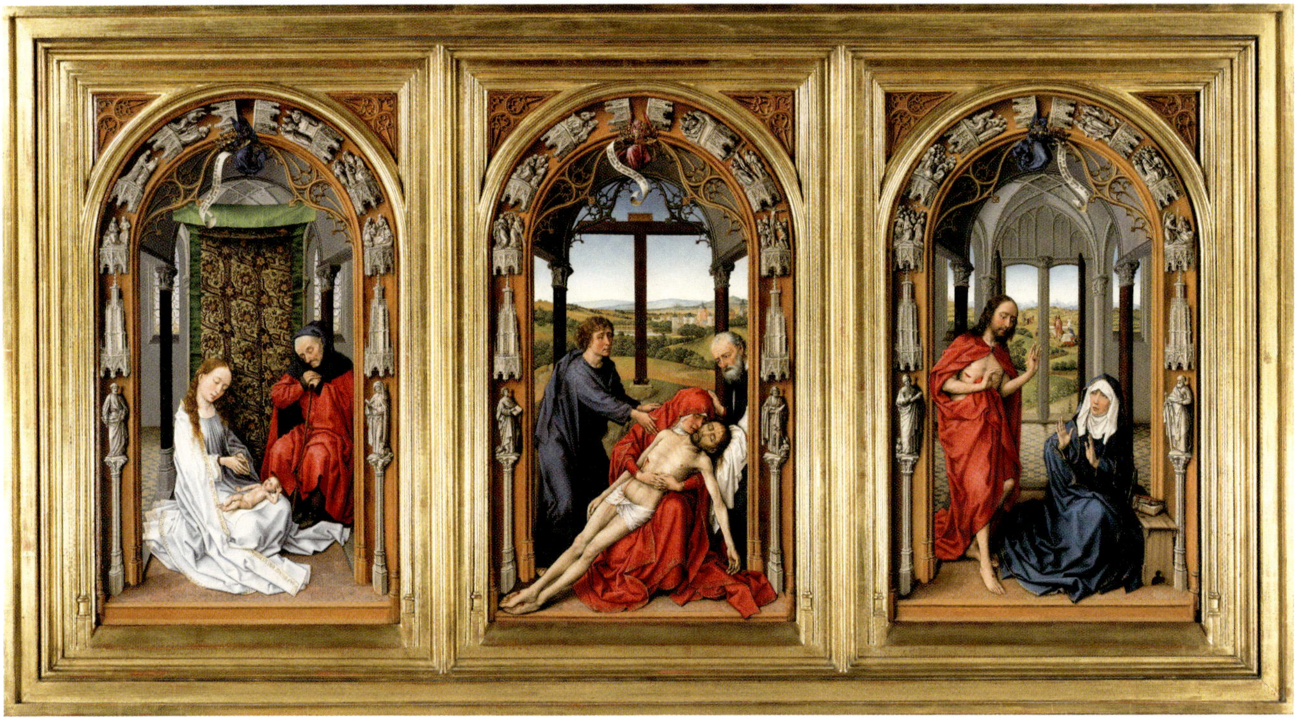

 ▷ 17 Rogier van der Weyden Miraflores Altarpiece Staatliche Museen, Gemäldegalerie, Berlin

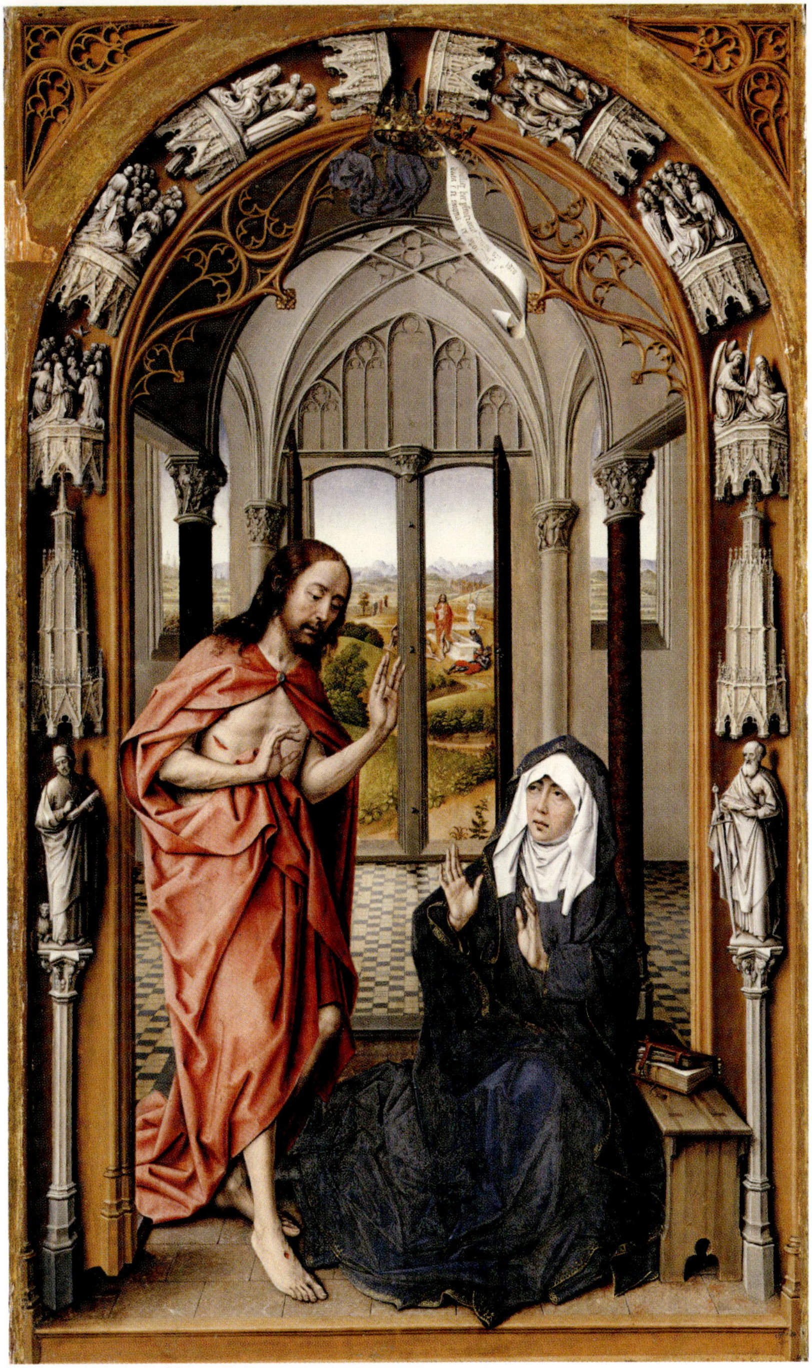

▷ 17 Juan de Flandes or Michel Sittow Christ Appearing to His Mother (Copy of the Miraflores Altarpiece)
The Metropolitan Museum of Art, New York

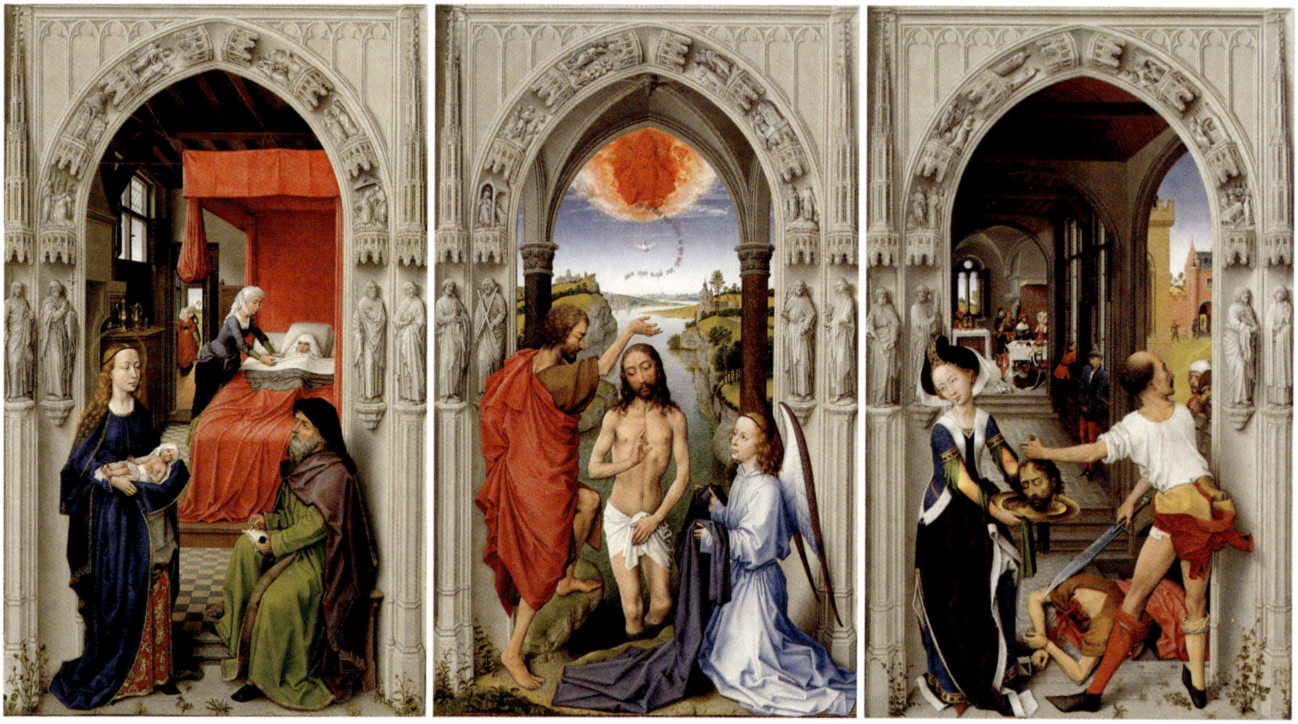



▷ 18 Rogier van der Weyden Saint John Altarpiece Staatliche Museen, Gemäldegalerie, Berlin

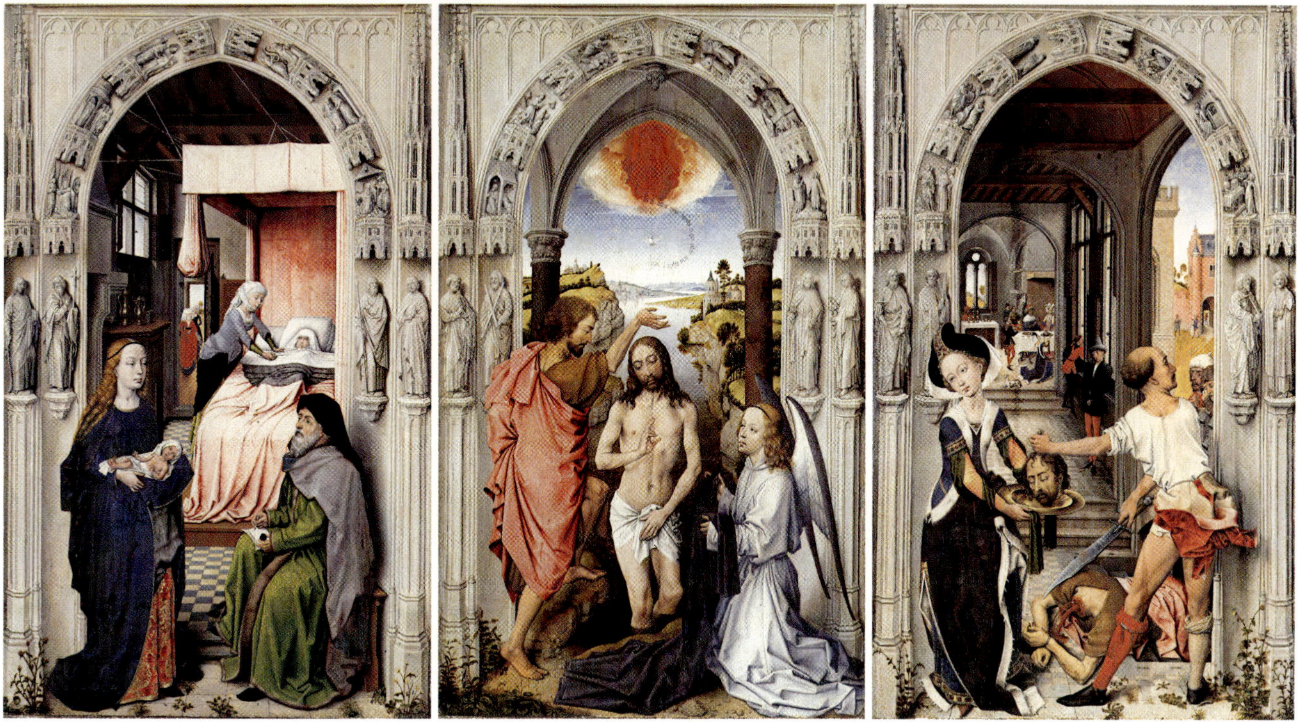

▷ 18 **Netherlandish Master, ca. 1500** Saint John Altarpiece (Copy after Rogier van der Weyden)
Städel Museum, Frankfurt am Main

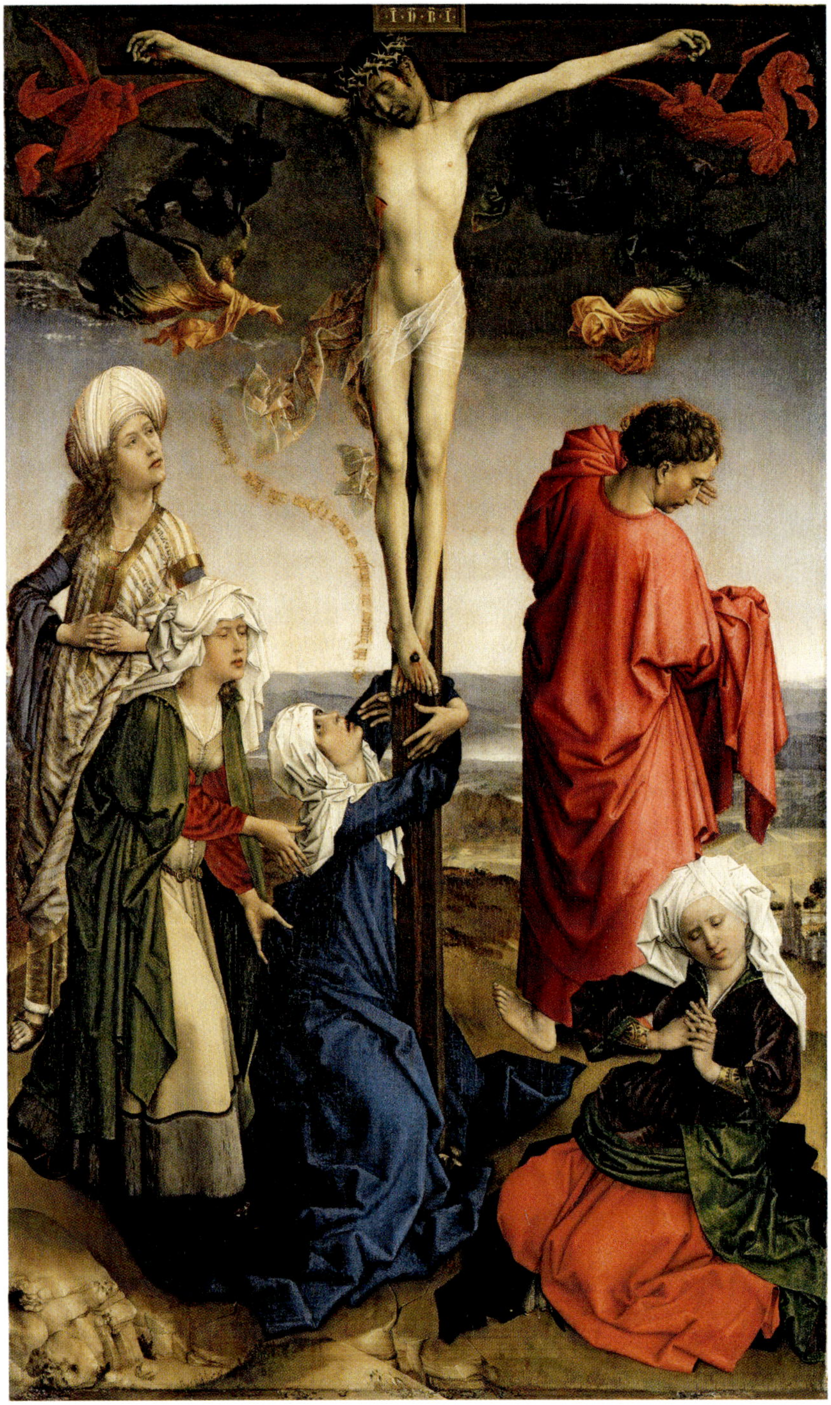



▷ 20 Workshop of Rogier van der Weyden The Crucifixion Staatliche Museen, Gemäldegalerie, Berlin

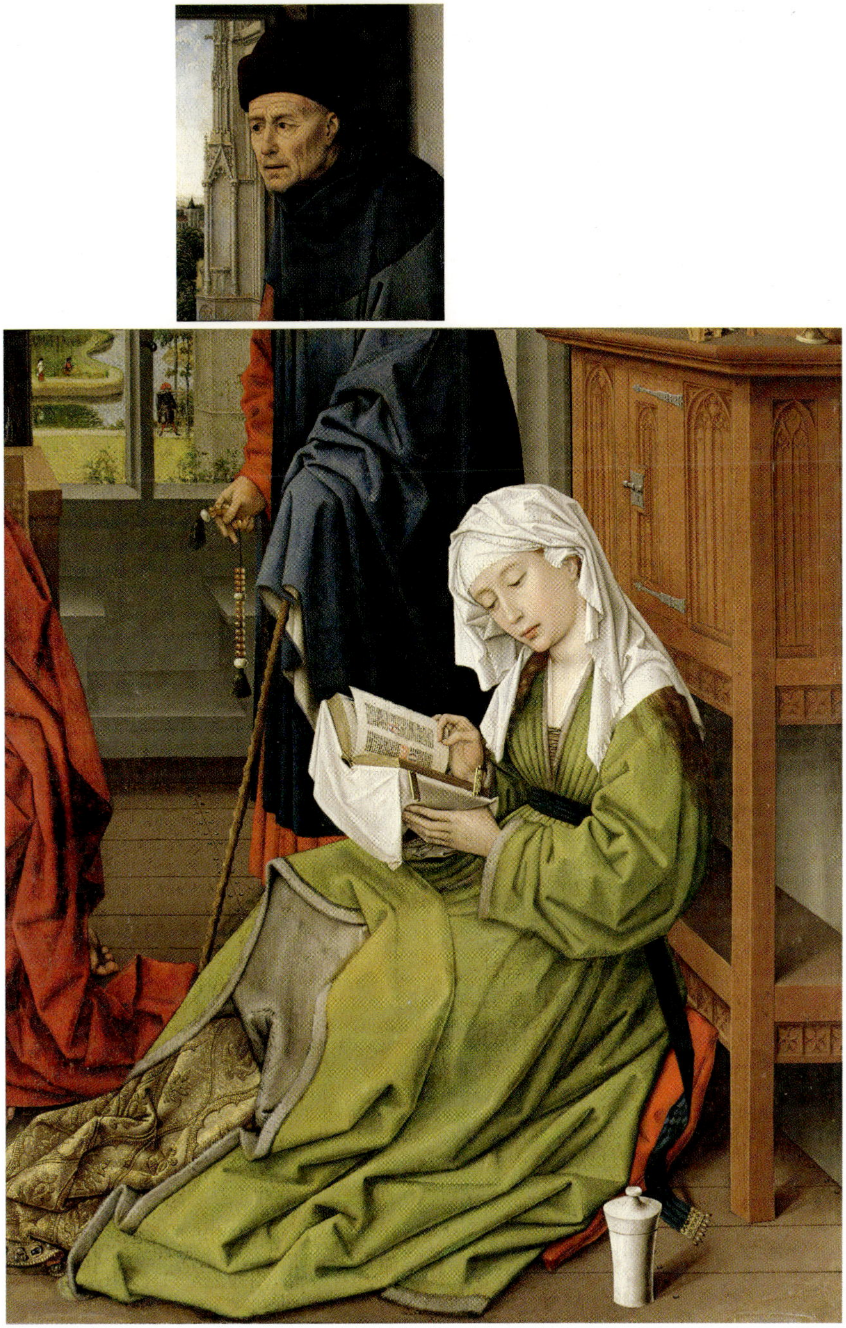

▷ 21 Workshop of Rogier van der Weyden (?) Fragments of an altarpiece:
Saint Joseph Museu Calouste Gulbenkian, Lisbon
Mary Magdalen Reading National Gallery, London

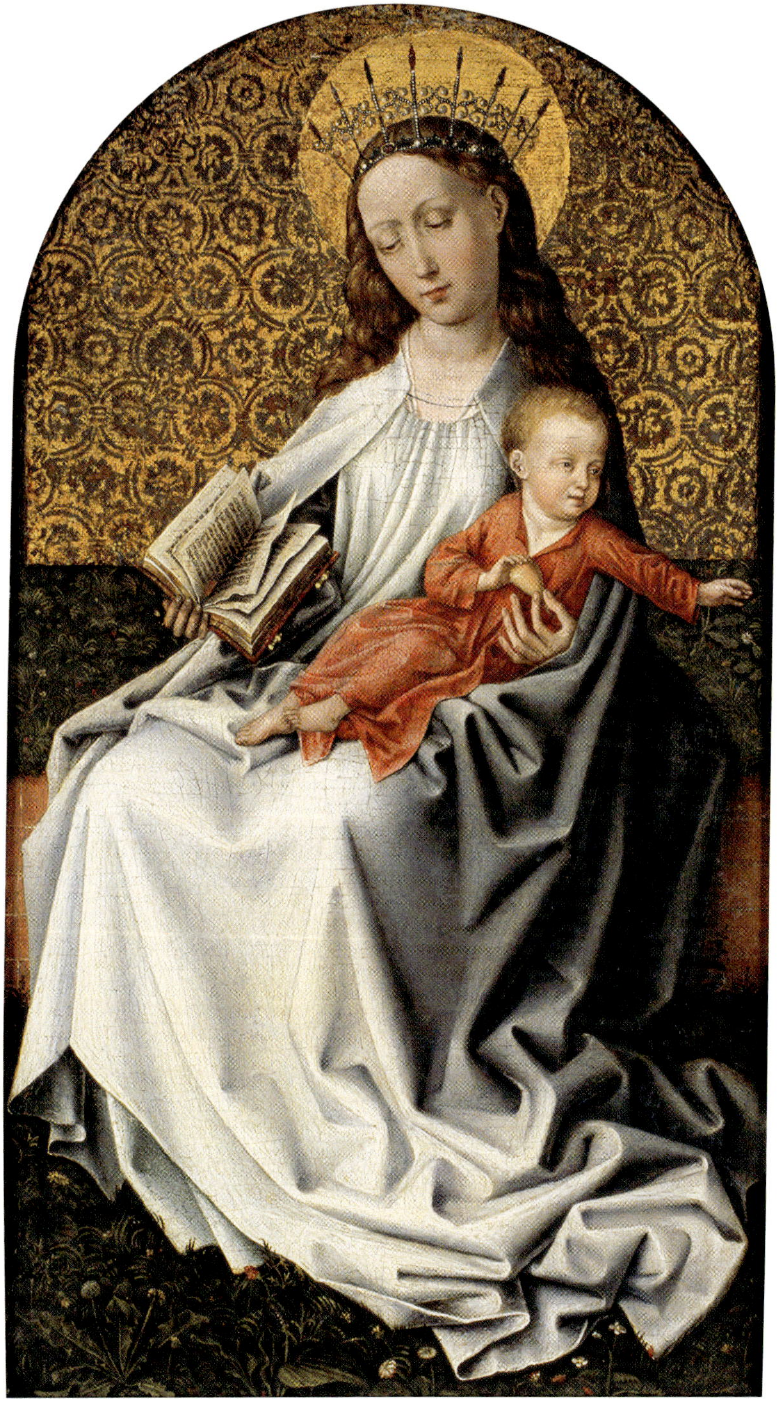

 ▷ 22 Workshop of Rogier van der Weyden (?) Madonna by a Grassy Bank Museum für Kunst und Kulturgeschichte, Dortmund

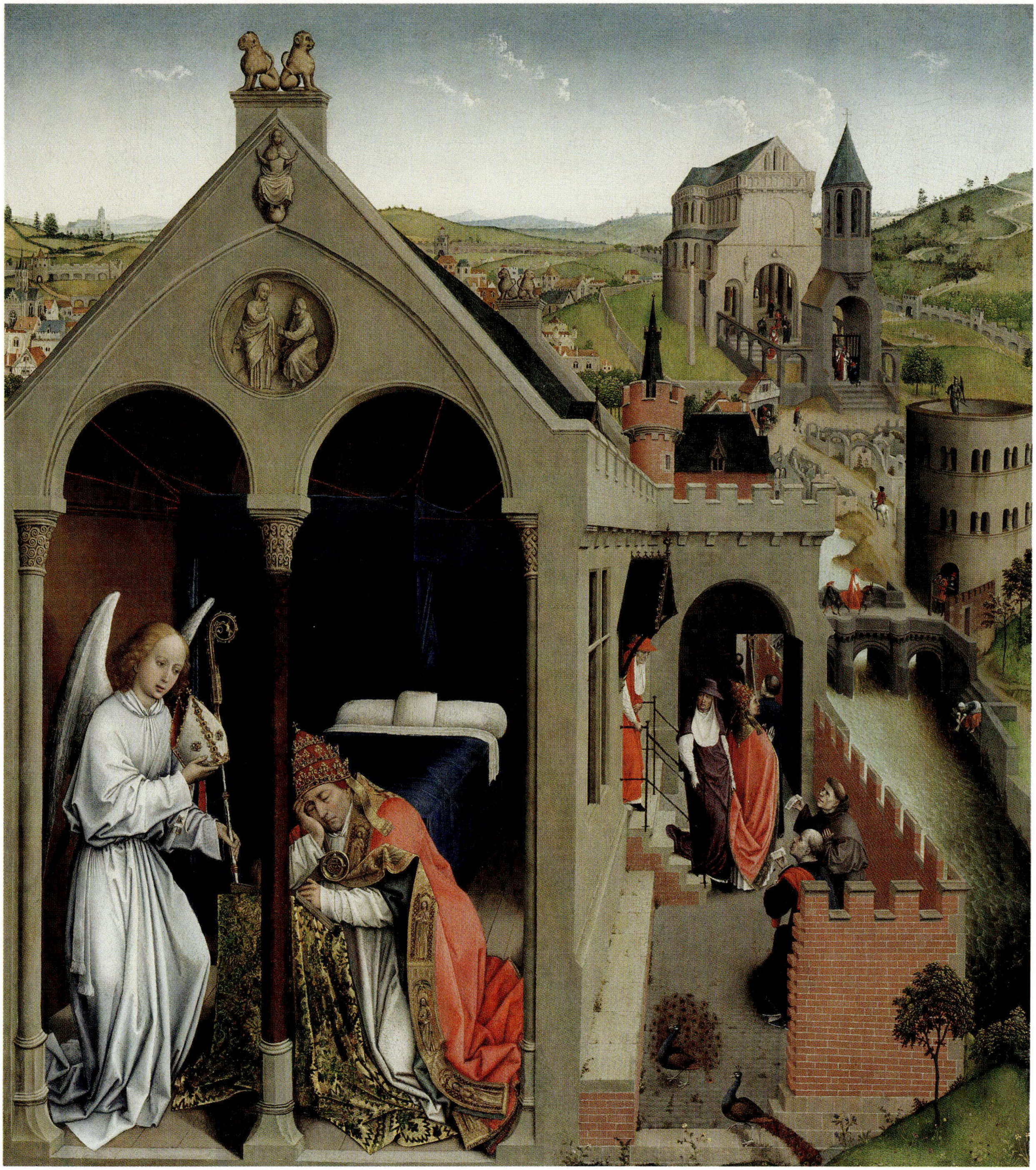

▷ 23 Workshop of Rogier van der Weyden The Dream of Pope Sergius The J. Paul Getty Museum, Los Angeles

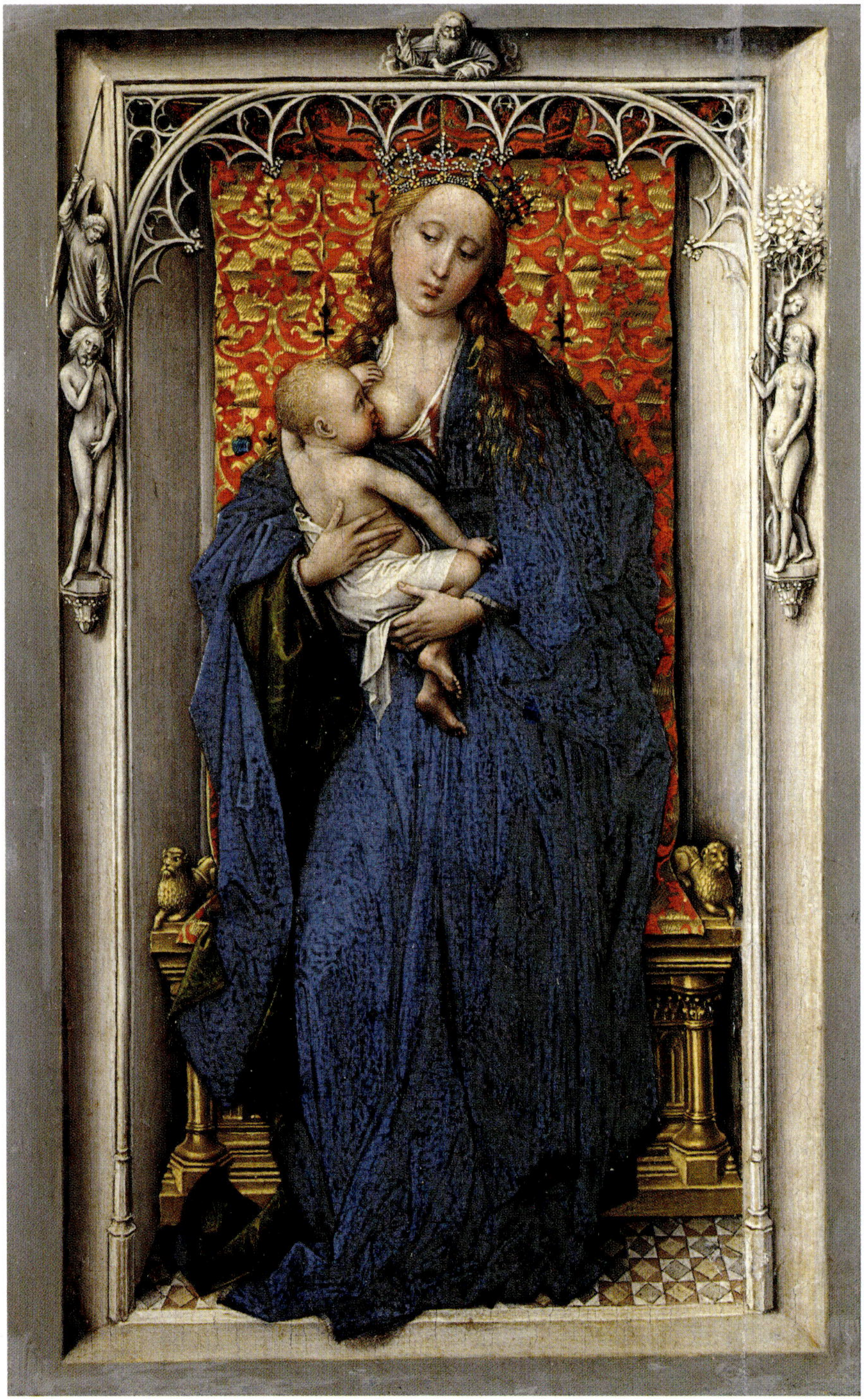

 ▷ 25 Workshop of Rogier van der Weyden The Madonna Nursing the Christ Child Kunsthistorisches Museum, Vienna

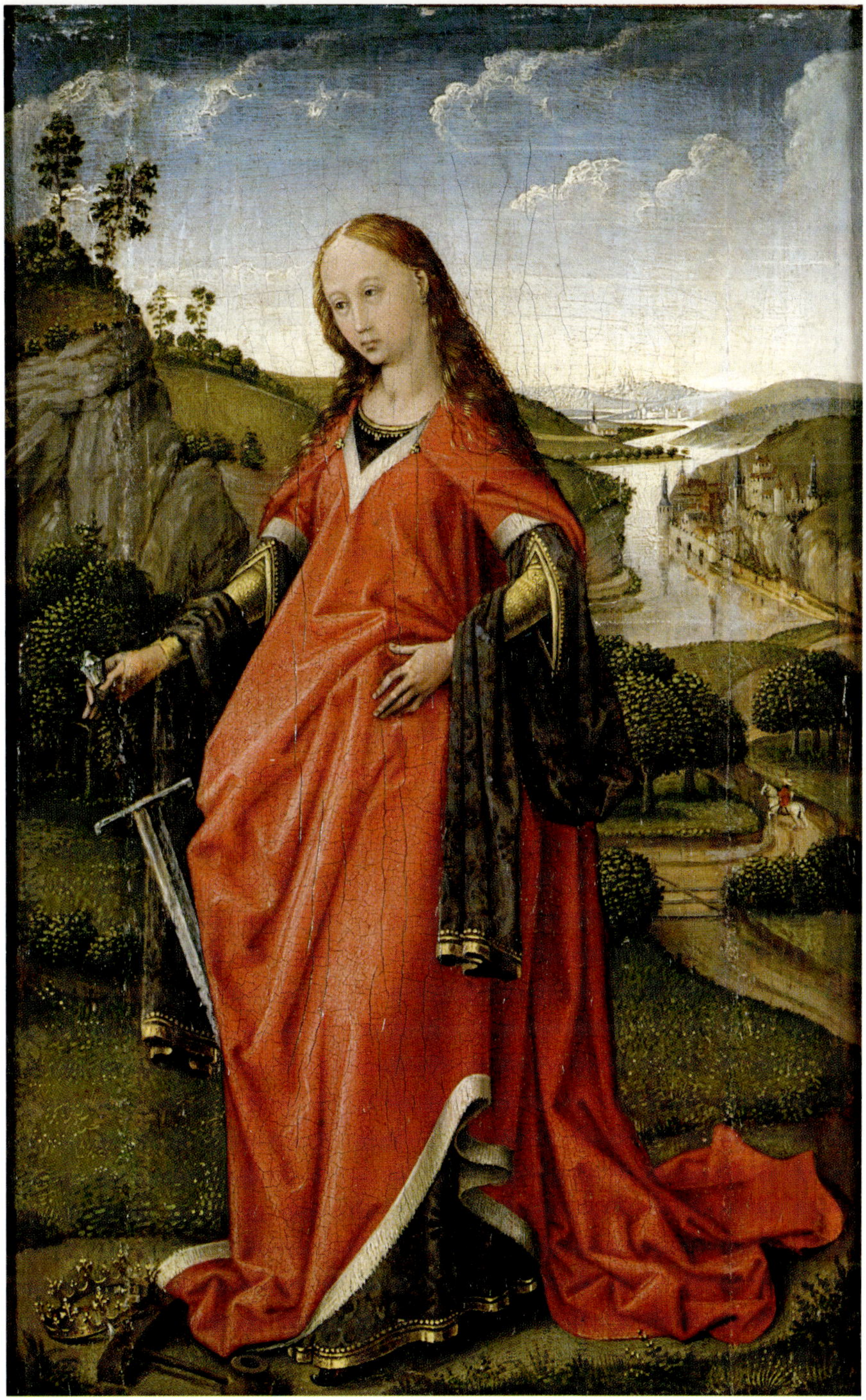

▷ 25 Workshop of Rogier van der Weyden Saint Catherine Kunsthistorisches Museum, Vienna

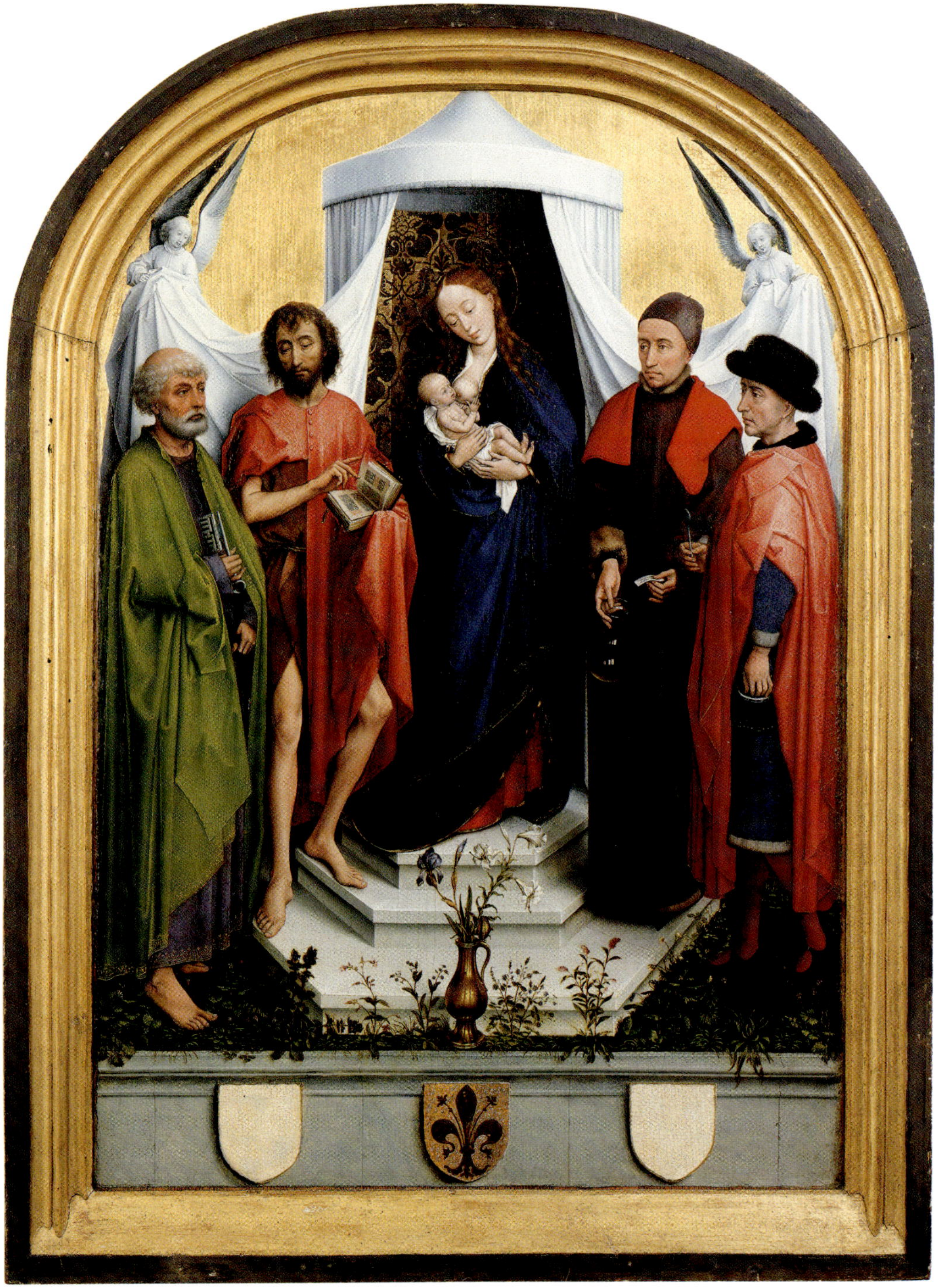

 ▷ 26 Rogier van der Weyden Medici Madonna Städel Museum, Frankfurt am Main

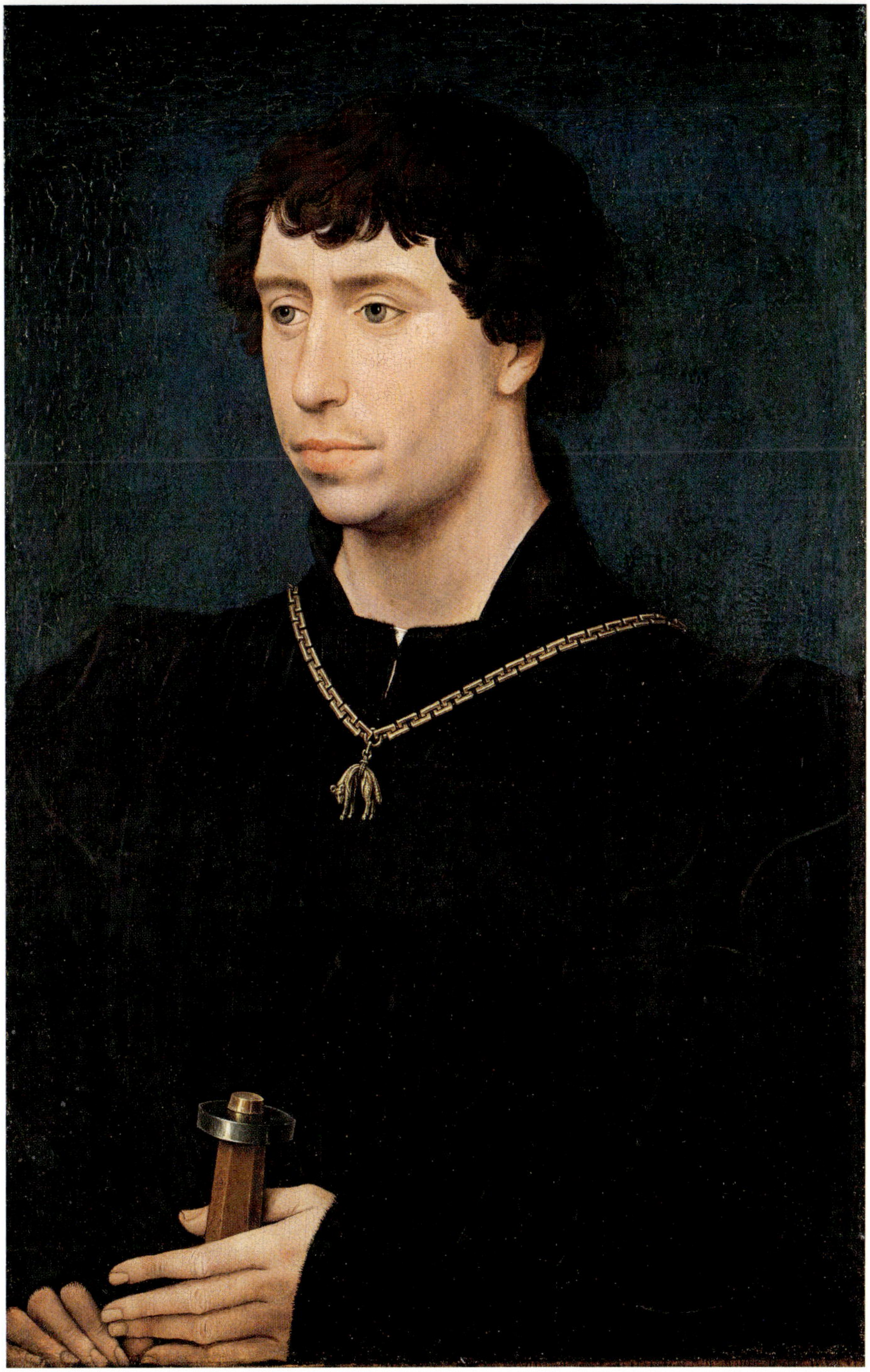

▷ 28 Workshop of Rogier van der Weyden (?) Portrait of Charles the Bold Staatliche Museen, Gemäldegalerie, Berlin

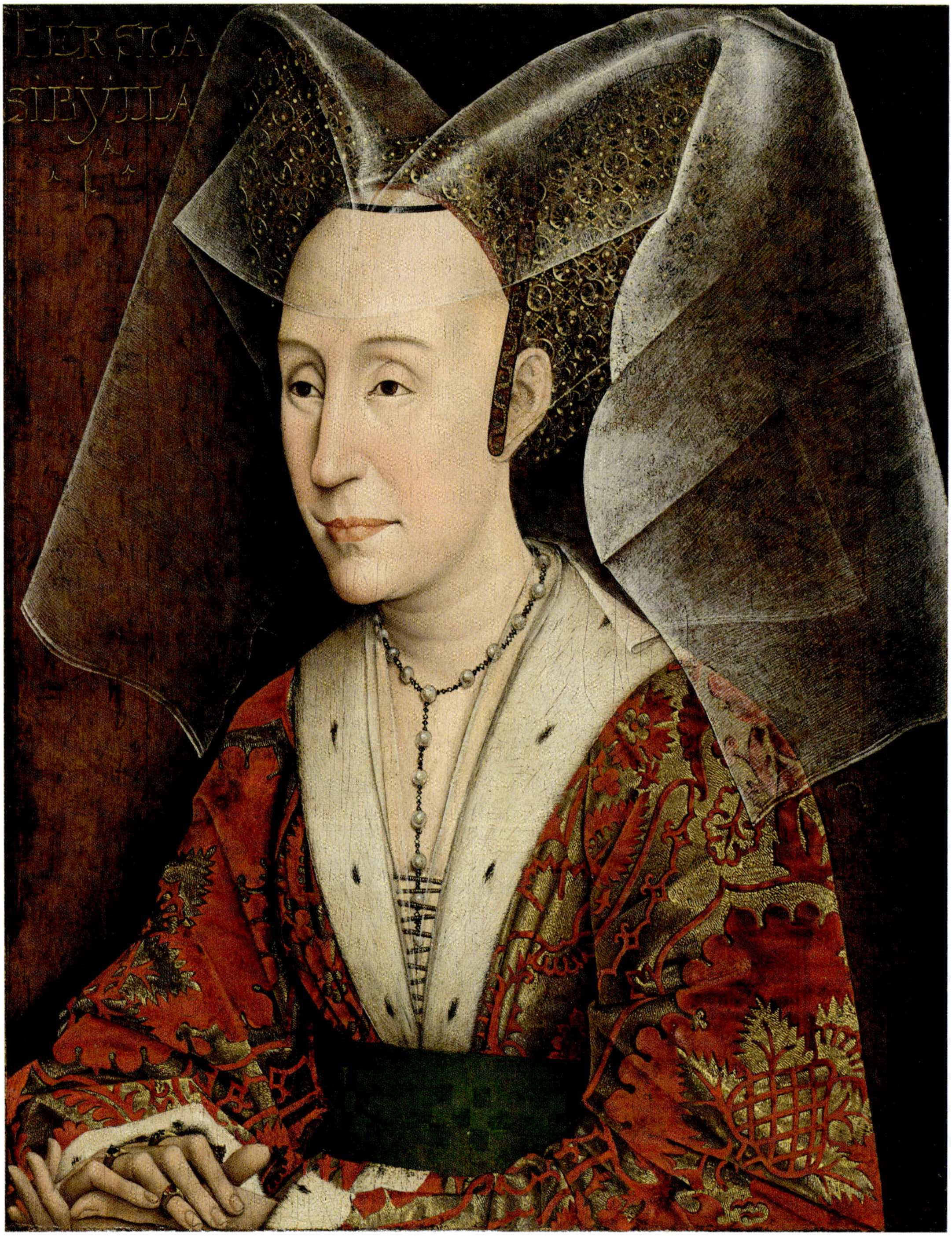



▷ 29 Workshop of Rogier van der Weyden Portrait of Isabella of Portugal The J. Paul Getty Museum, Los Angeles

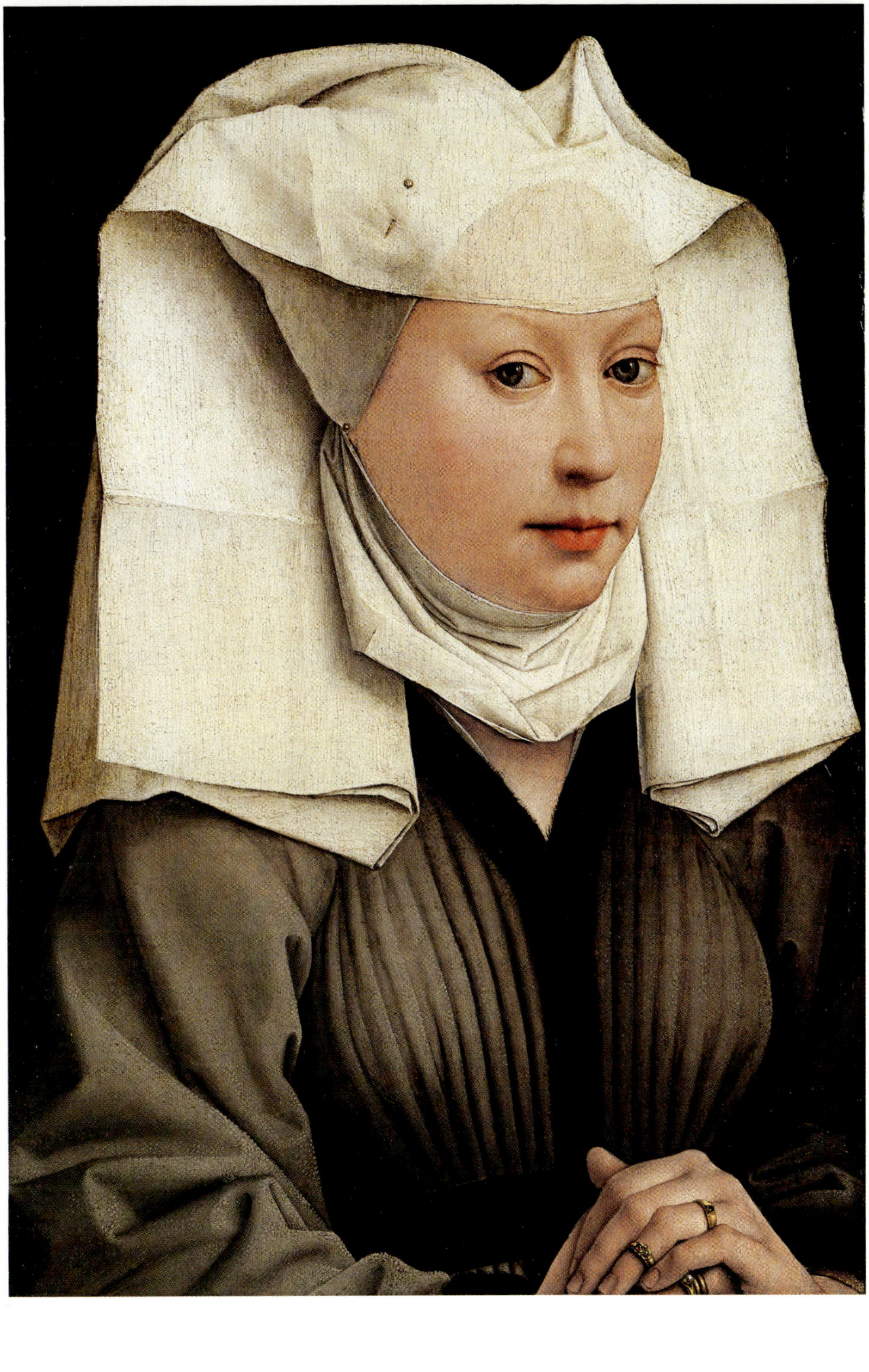

▷ 30 Rogier van der Weyden Portrait of a Young Woman Staatliche Museen, Gemäldegalerie, Berlin

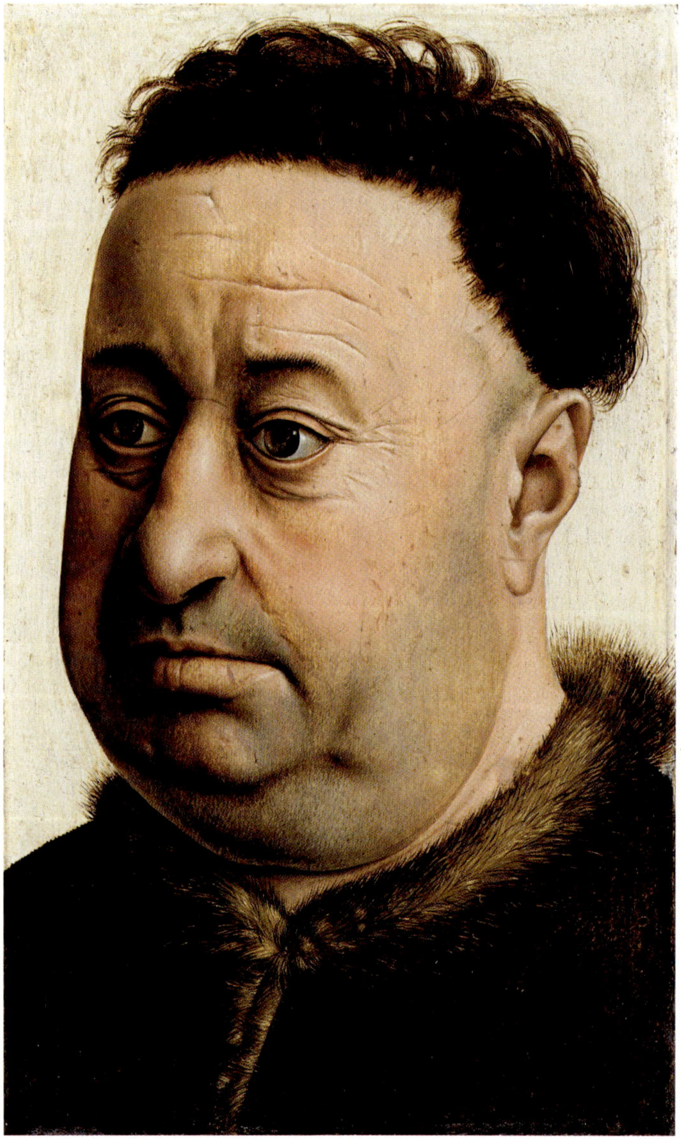

▷ 31 Master of Flémalle (Rogier van der Weyden?) Portrait of a Stout Man
Staatliche Museen, Gemäldegalerie, Berlin

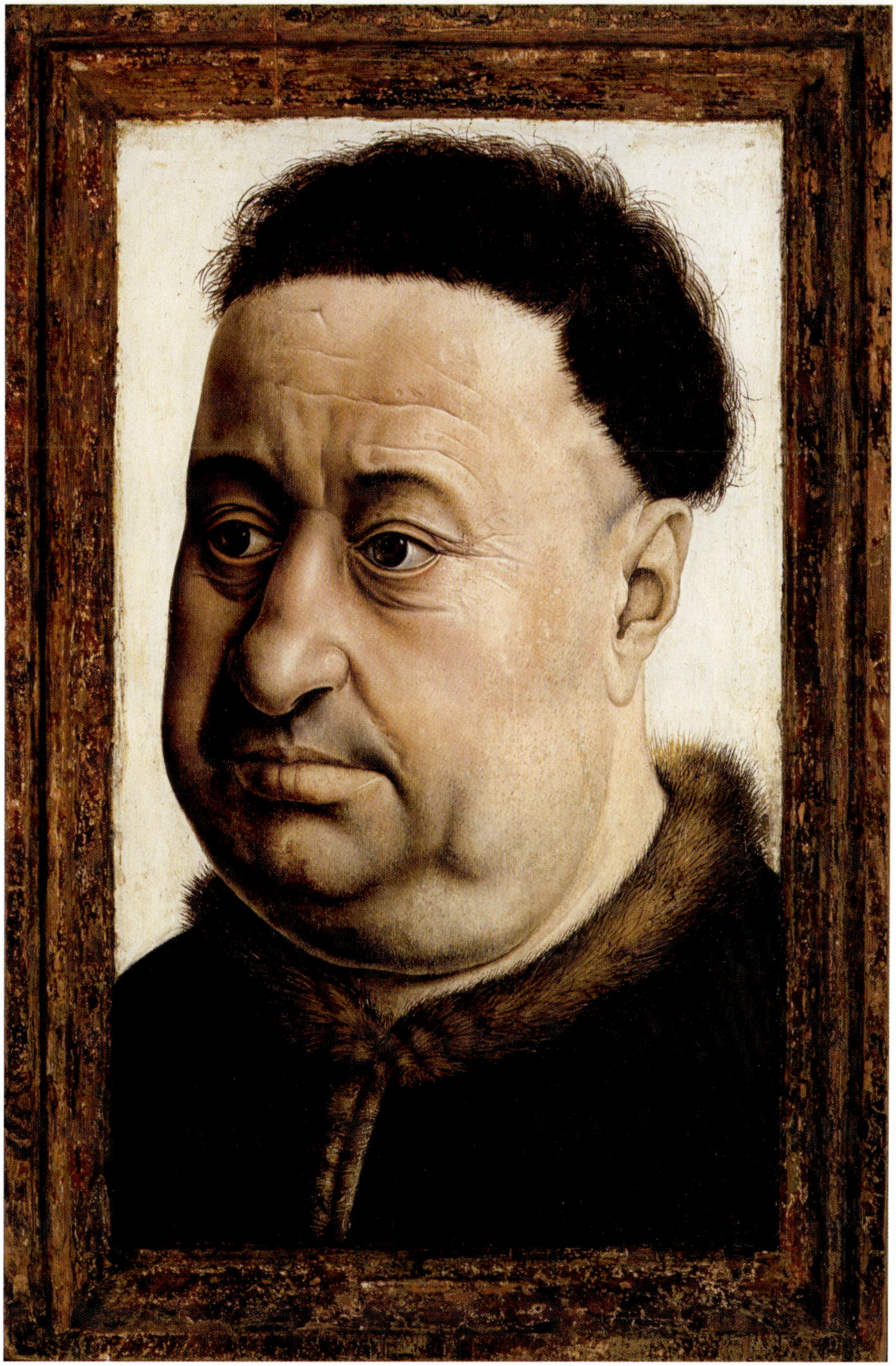

⊳ 31 Copy after the Master of Flémalle (Rogier van der Weyden?) Portrait of a Stout Man
Museo Thyssen-Bornemisza, Madrid

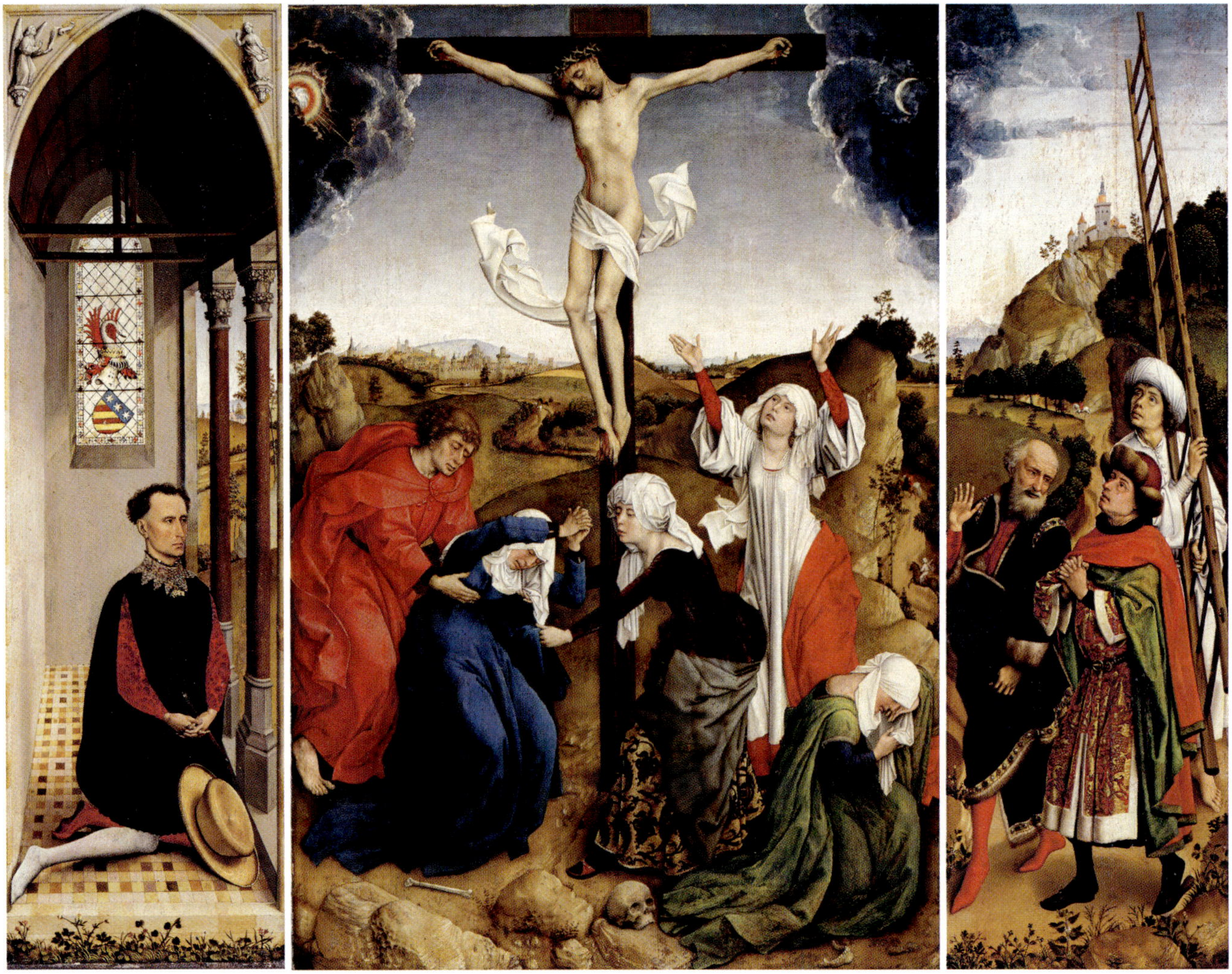

 ▷ 32 Workshop of Rogier van der Weyden The Crucifixion (Abegg Triptych) Abegg-Stiftung, Riggisberg

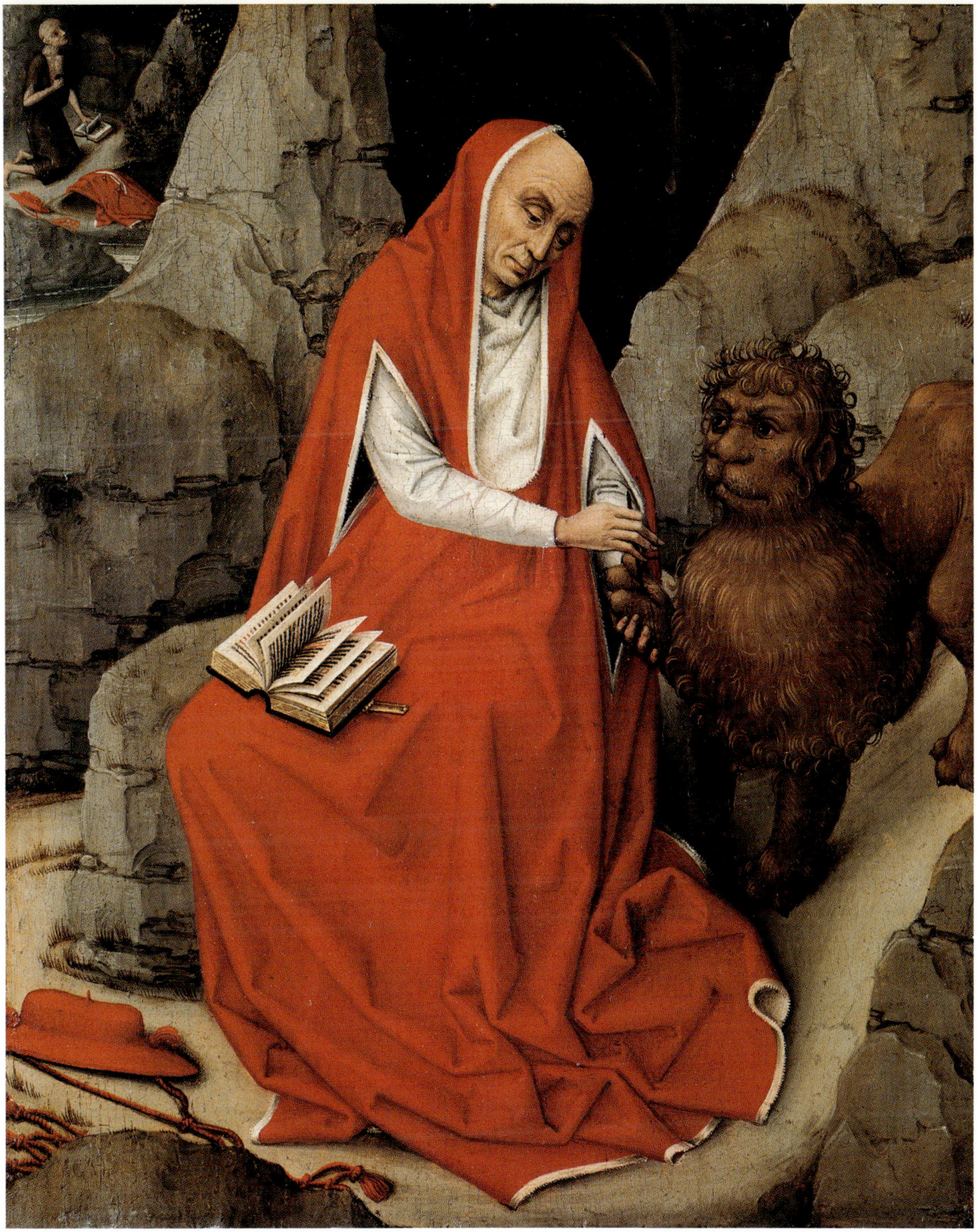

▷ 33 Workshop of Rogier van der Weyden (?) Saint Jerome with the Lion Detroit Institute of Arts, Detroit

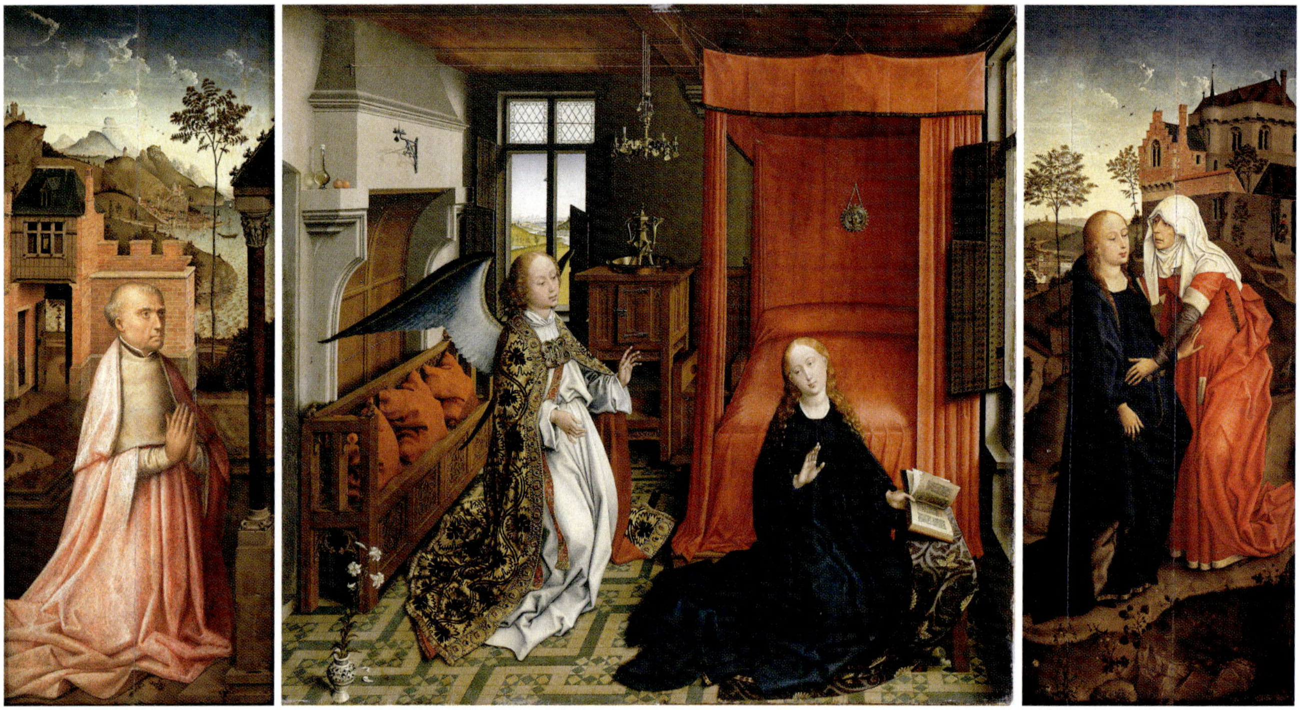

▷ 34 Workshop of Rogier van der Weyden (?)

Triptych of Saint Mary:
Donor Galleria Sabauda, Turin
The Annunciation Musée du Louvre, Paris
The Visitation Galleria Sabauda, Turin

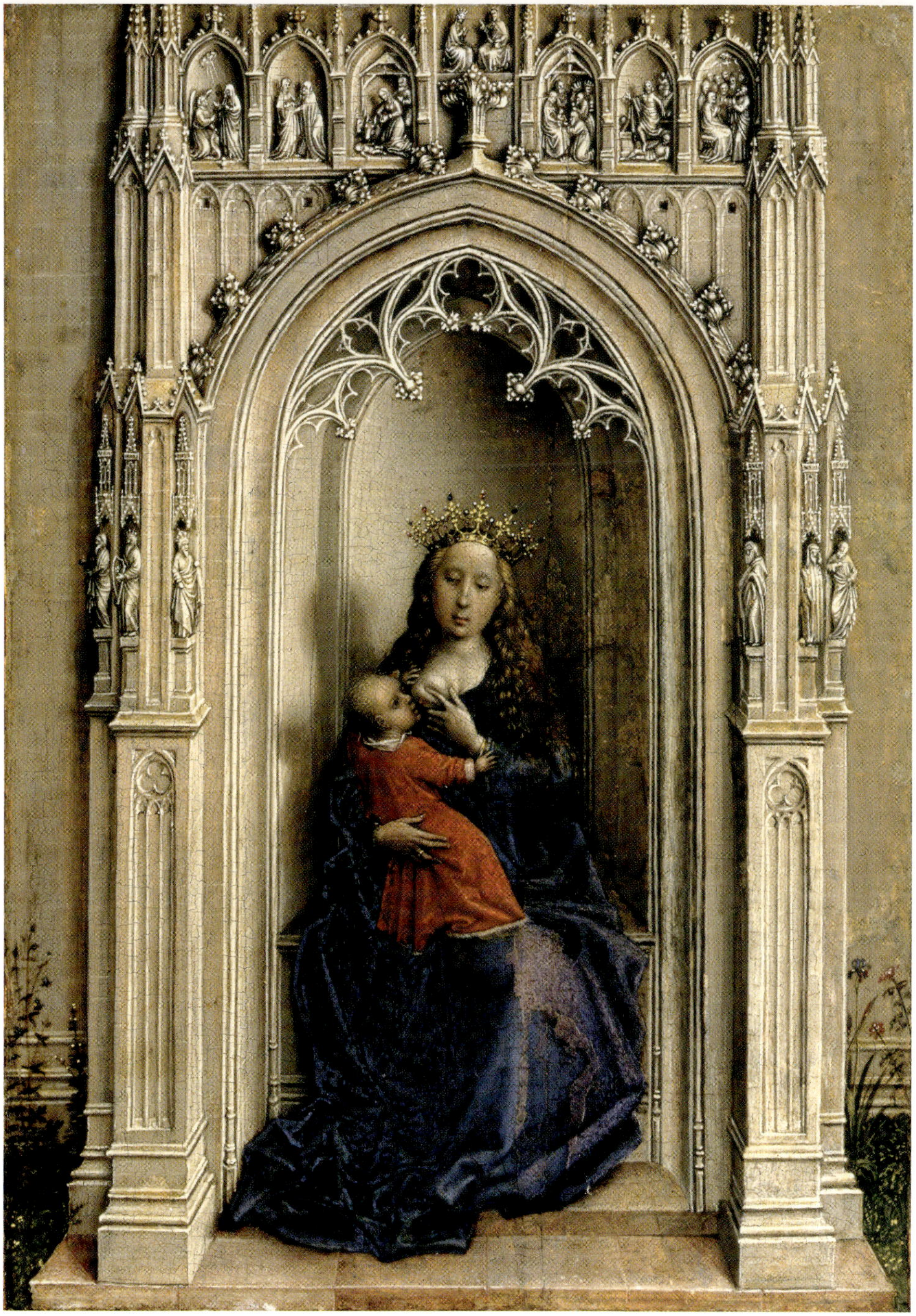

▷ 35 Workshop of Rogier van der Weyden (?) Recto of a diptych wing: Enthroned Madonna and Child Museo Thyssen-Bornemisza, Madrid

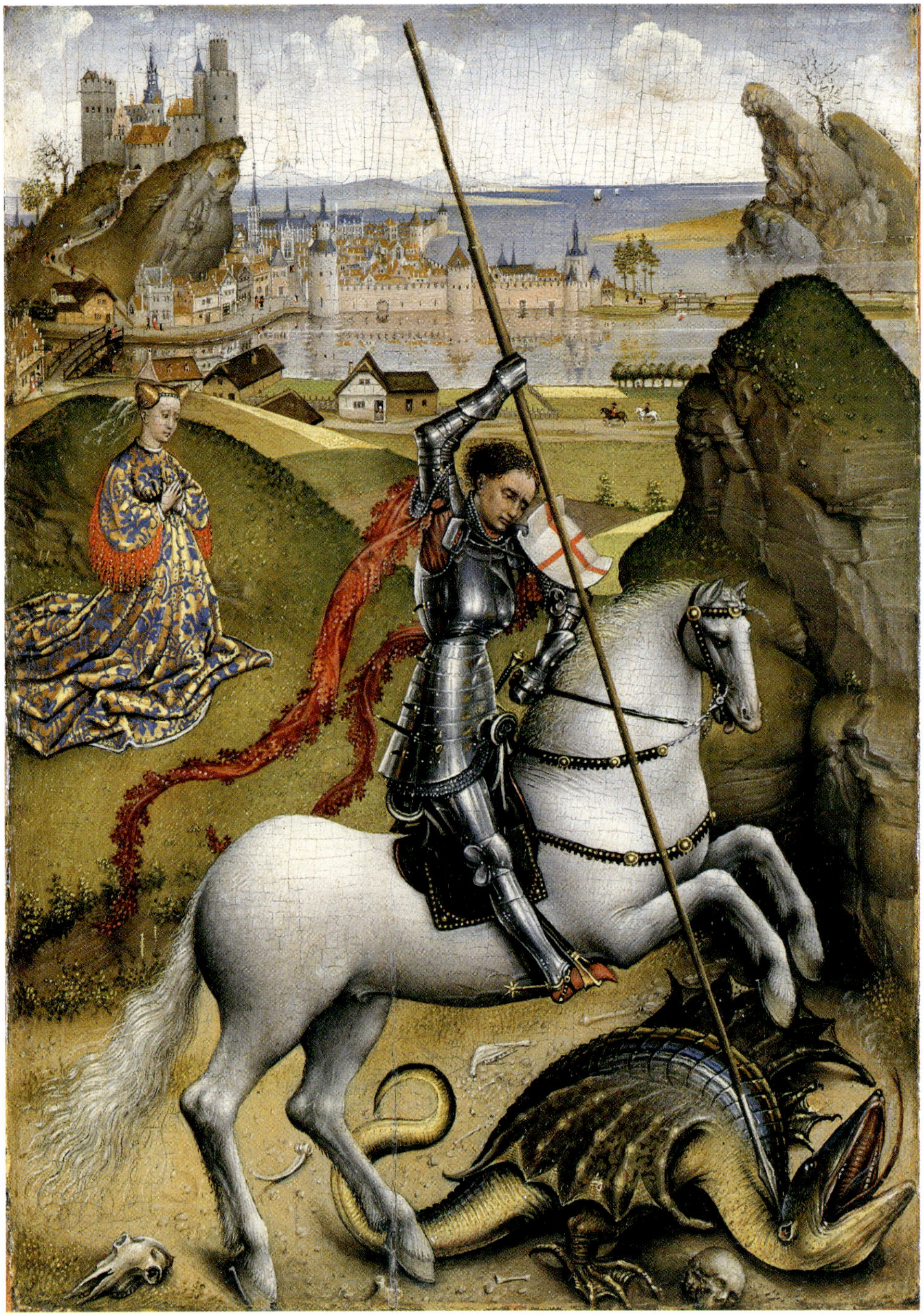

▷ 35 Workshop of Rogier van der Weyden (?) Verso of a diptych wing: Saint George and the Dragon National Gallery of Art, Washington, D.C.

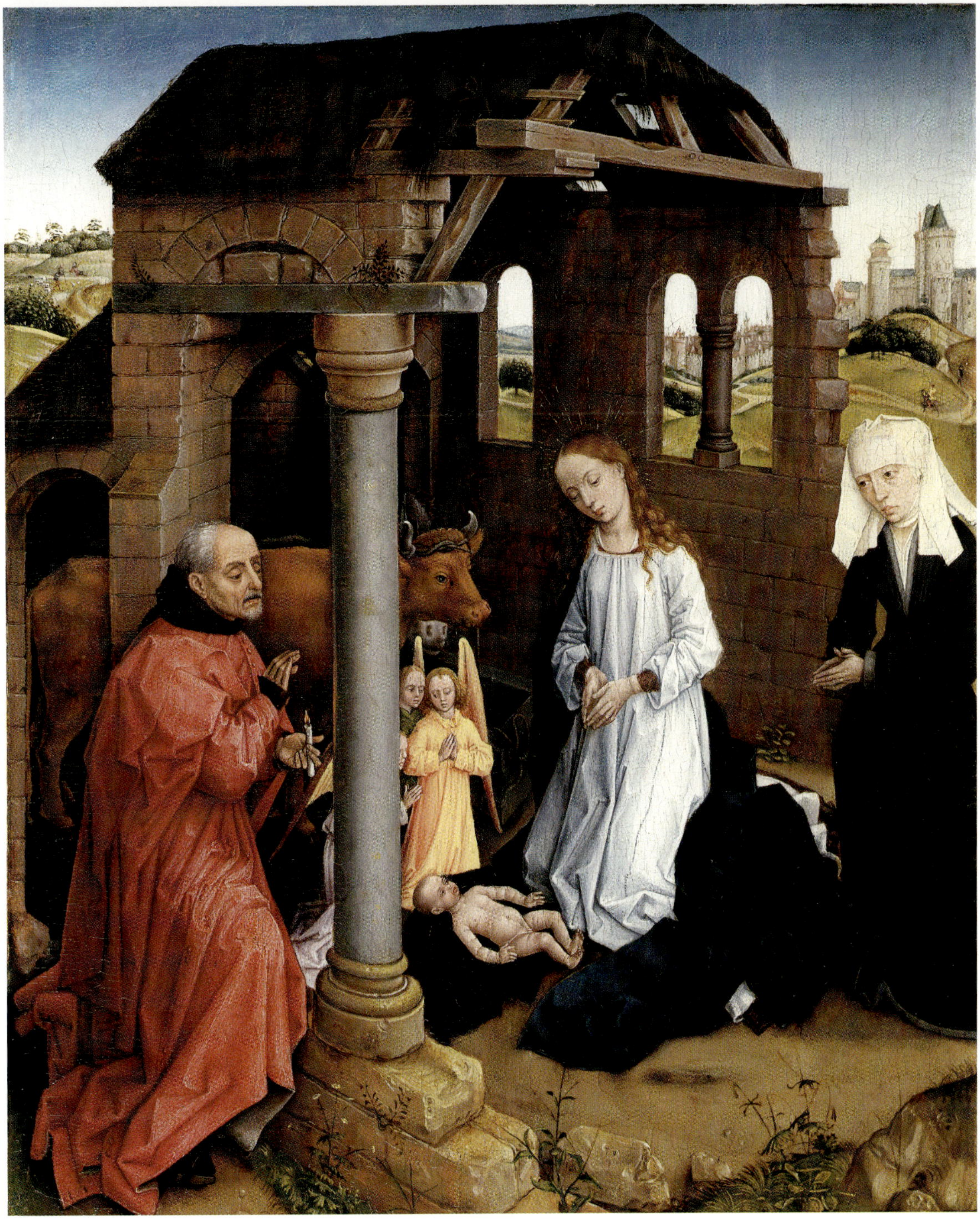

▷ 36 Workshop of Rogier van der Weyden The Birth of Christ with a Female Donor Marks-Thomée collection, Germany

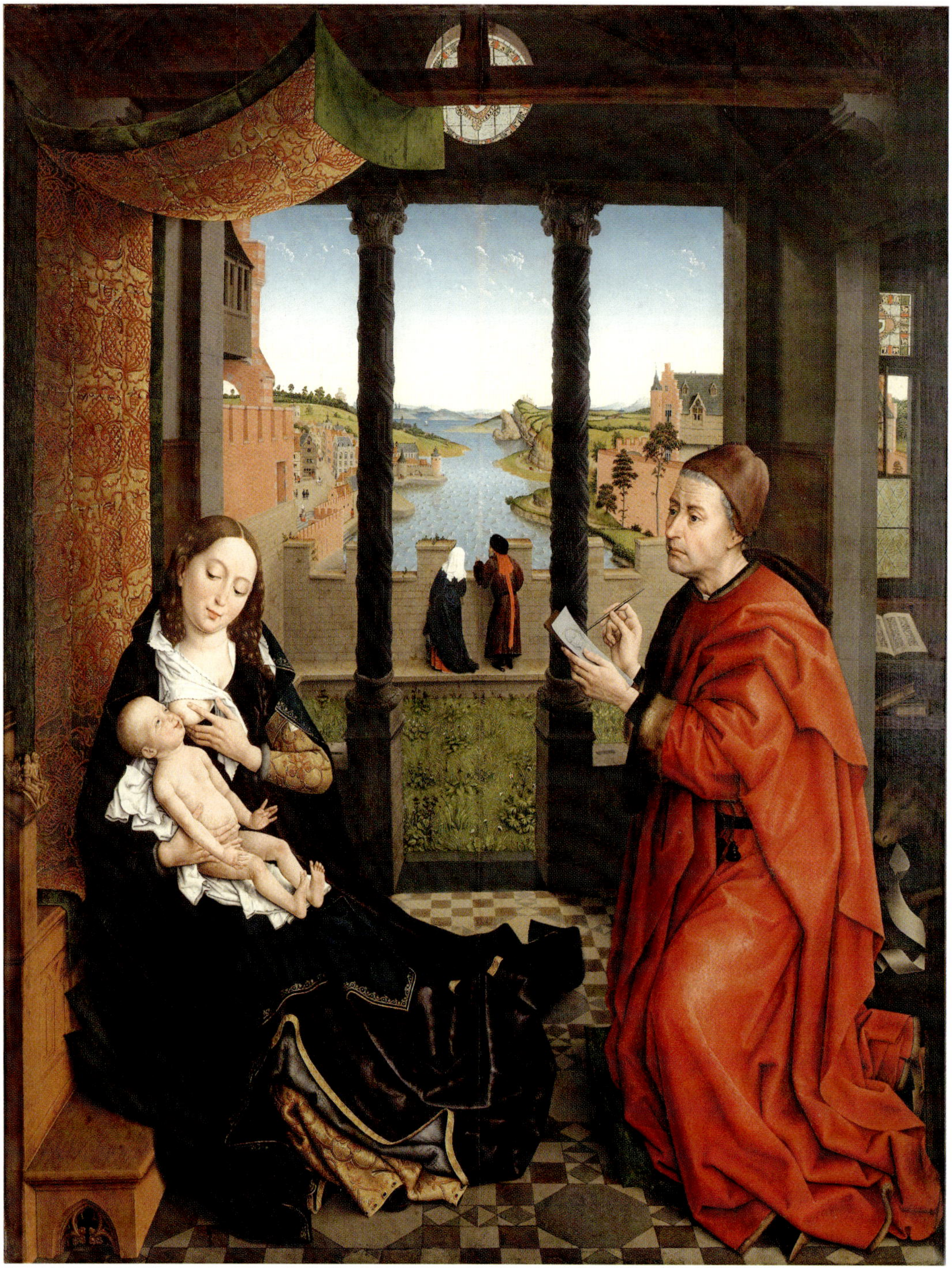



▷ 37 Copy after Rogier van der Weyden Saint Luke Drawing the Madonna Groeningemuseum, Bruges

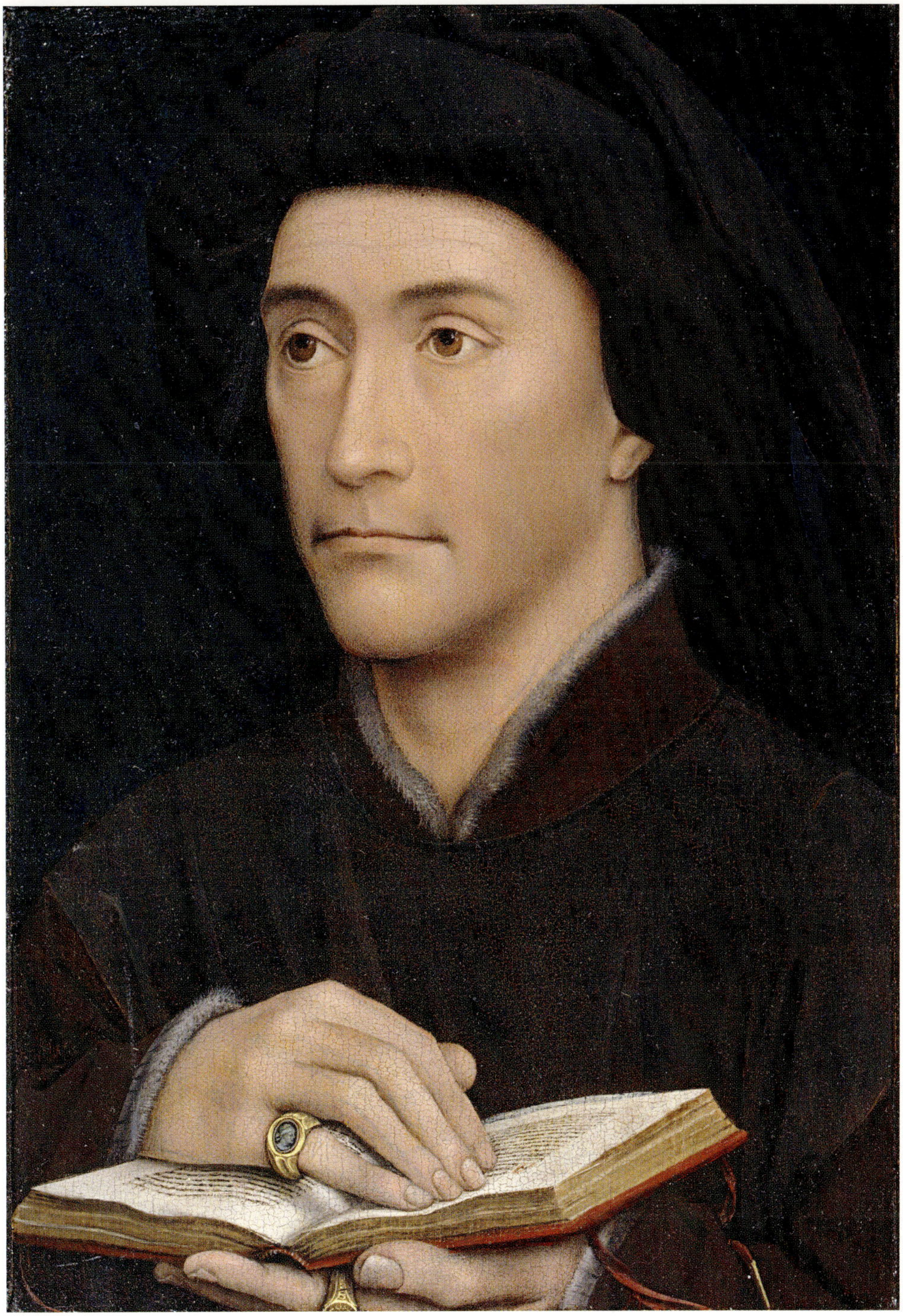

▷ 38 Workshop of Rogier van der Weyden Portrait of a Man Courtauld Institute Art Gallery, London

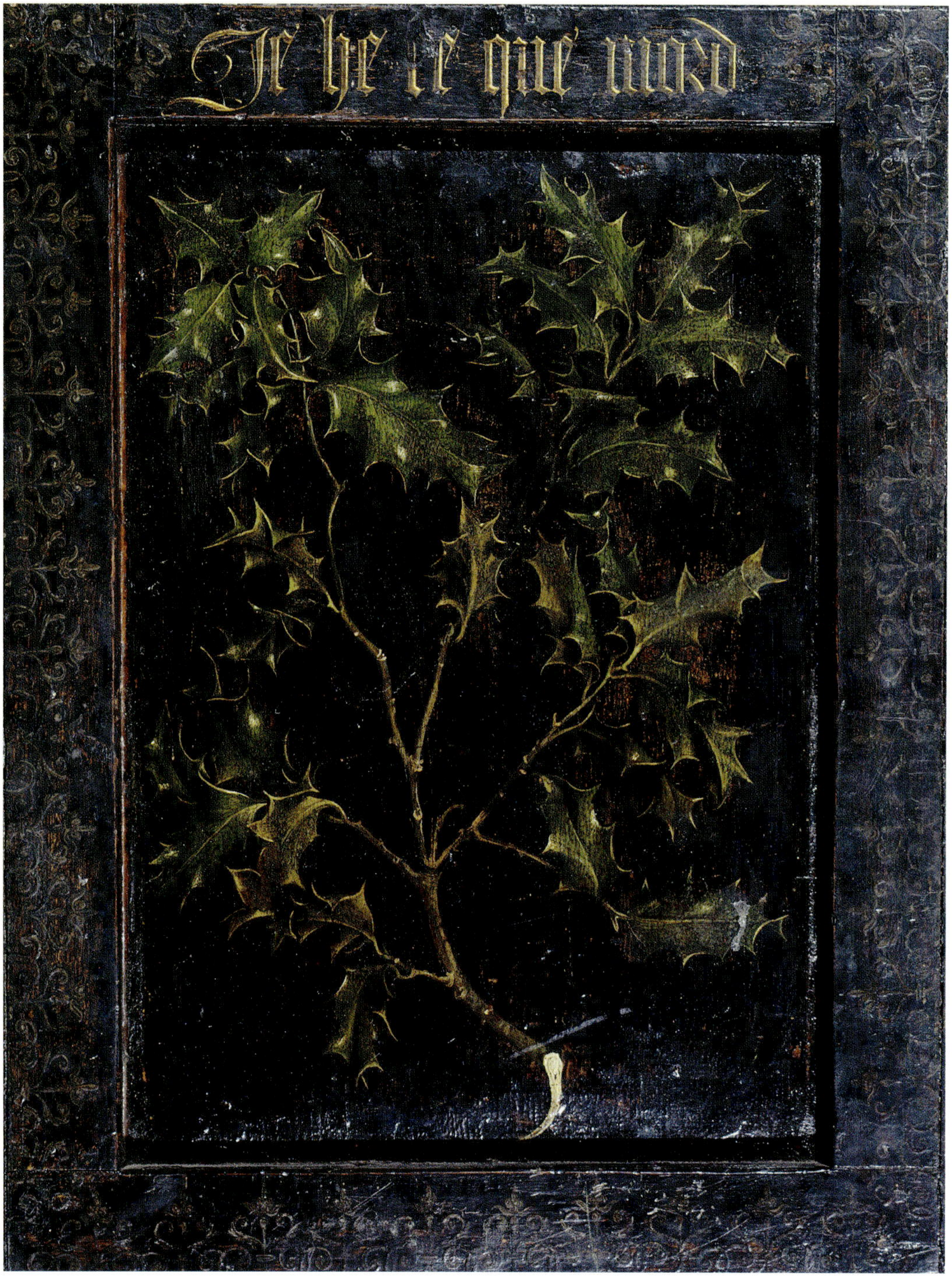




▷ 38 Workshop of Rogier van der Weyden Portrait of a Man (verso) Courtauld Institute Art Gallery, London

## Image Credits

Abegg-Stiftung, Riggisberg, ©1999, Christoph von Viràg: p. 38
Artothek, Weilheim, Ursula Edelmann: pp. 14–16, 25
Bildarchiv Preussischer Kulturbesitz, Berlin / RNM, Musée du Louvre, Paris, Gérard Blot: p. 40 (central panel)
Detroit Institute of Arts, Detroit: p. 39
Fundação Calouste Gulbenkian, Museo Calouste Gulbenkian, Arquivo Fotográfico, Lisbon: p. 27
Galleria Sabauda, Turin, Ernani Orcorte: p. 40 (wing)
Groeningemuseum – ©Lukas – Art in Flanders VZW, Bruges: p. 44
The J. Paul Getty Museum, Imaging Lab, Los Angeles: pp. 29, 34
Kunsthistorisches Museum, Vienna: pp. 30–31
Marks-Thomée collection, Germany: p. 43
The Metropolitan Museum of Art, The Cloisters Collection, New York, 1956 (56.70a–c)
Image ©The Metropolitan Museum of Art: p. 7
The Metropolitan Museum of Art, New York, The Bequest of Michael Dreicer, 1921 (22.60.58)
Image ©The Metropolitan Museum of Art: p. 23
Musée des Beaux-Arts, Dijon, François Jay: p. 8
Museo Nacional del Prado, Madrid: pp. 9–10
Museo Thyssen-Bornemisza, Madrid: pp. 19, 37, 41
Museum für Kunst- und Kulturgeschichte, Dortmund, Madeleine-Annette Albrecht: p. 28
National Gallery of Art, Department of Visual Services, Washington, D. C.: pp. 11, 42
La Parisienne de Photographie, Paris, Delphine Desveaux: p. 21
Philadelphia Museum of Art, Philadelphia, Graydon Wood: p. 17
Ro Scan, Brussels, J. Geleyns: p. 6
Rühl und Bormann, Darmstadt: p. 32
The Samuel Courtauld Trust, Courtauld Institute Art Gallery, London: pp. 45–46
Staatliche Museen, Gemäldegalerie, Berlin, Jörg P. Anders: pp. 5, 18, 20, 24, 36
Staatliche Museen, Gemäldegalerie, Berlin, Volker H. Schneider: pp. 22, 28, 33, 35
The State Hermitage, St. Petersburg: p. 12
Bernard Terlay CPA, Aix-en-Provence: p. 13

This catalogue is published in conjunction with the exhibition
The Master of Flémalle and Rogier van der Weyden
Städel Museum, Frankfurt am Main, November 21, 2008 – February 22, 2009
Staatliche Museen, Gemäldegalerie, Berlin, March 20 – June 21, 2009

Audio CD
Conception and texts: Ursula Vorwerk
Managing editor: Oliver Gustke
English translations: Andrew Boreham
Narrator: J. J. Gordon
Director: Steffi Herrmann
Producer: Lutz Oldemeier
CD production: KMS Kafitz Medienservice GmbH, Elsdorf-Heppendorf

CD Booklet
Copyediting: Tas Skorupa, Krystina Stermole
Graphic design: KOMA AMOK, Stuttgart
Production: Stefanie Langner, Hatje Cantz
Typeface: Monotype Grotesque (Frank Hinman Pierpont)
Paper: LuxoSamtoffset, 170 g/m²
Reproductions: Repromayer, Reutlingen
Printing and binding: Kösel GmbH & Co. KG, Altusried
Published by:
Hatje Cantz Verlag, Zeppelinstrasse 32, 73760 Ostfildern, Germany
Tel. +49 711 4405-200, Fax +49 711 4405-220, www.hatjecantz.com

Hatje Cantz books are available internationally at selected bookstores.
For more information about our distribution partners please visit our homepage at www.hatjecantz.com

ISBN 978-3-7757-2365-7 (English)
ISBN 978-3-7757-2364-0 (German)

Printed in Germany



Cover illustration:
Rogier van der Weyden, *Portrait of a Young Woman,* Staatliche Museen, Gemäldegalerie, Berlin

GEMA